LETTING GO

Without Giving Up

CS Larsen

KnowledgeGain Inc.

ISBN: 978-0-9779844-3-5

Cover design by: CS Larsen
Library of Congress Control Number: 2018675309
Printed in the United States of America

CONTENTS

CHAPTER 1 - THE BENEFITS OF LETTING GO

There are many benefits to learning how to let go, both for our mental and emotional well-being and personal growth and development.

One of the most important benefits of letting go is that it can help us reduce stress and anxiety. Holding onto something, whether it's a past mistake or a grudge against someone, can create a constant undercurrent of stress and tension in your life. You can release that tension and find greater peace by learning to let go - without giving up.

You can also be bent on a desired outcome in the future, which too will inhibit your growth. Hoping for a specific job, relationship, or a new material item may not necessarily provide you happiness. All the toys and money in the world may not bring you joy. Countless studies have shown that those who make it rich through hard work or winning the lottery do not make their lives complete. Yes, it can make it easier from a financial perspective, but nothing in your life matters unless you find happiness in the here and now.

Letting go can also help us improve our relationships with others. When you're not holding onto anger, resentment, or hurt, you're more able to connect with others from a place of compassion and understanding. This can lead to stronger, more authentic relationships with ourselves and those around us.

In addition to these benefits, letting go can also create space for new opportunities and experiences to come into your life. When you're not holding onto the past, you're able to be more present in the moment and open to what the future may bring. This can lead to exciting new possibilities and adventures you may not have considered otherwise.

As stated, letting go can be a powerful personal growth and transformation tool. By breaking free from old patterns and beliefs, you can create a positive world in which to live and provide the best avenue to being authentic. This process may be challenging at times, but it can lead to incredible growth and transformation, both personally and spiritually.

Letting go can also increase your self-awareness. By recognizing when you're holding onto something that's negative, you can become more aware of your thoughts, emotions, and beliefs and how they impact your life.

Resilience and energy can also be a benefit of letting go. When you're able to let go of bad emotions and beliefs, you become more adaptable and better able to handle difficult situations in your life. You are not attached to "oh no, here we go again" thinking. Let the situation or thoughts come and go – be the great observer of your mind, not a prisoner of it.

Letting go can also increase your creativity and innovation. By releasing old patterns and beliefs, you create space for new ideas and perspectives, which can help us come up with creative solutions to problems. Open your mind to alternative possibilities and use critical thinking to determine the appropriate outcomes.

And finally, letting go can also improve your physical health. When you're holding onto negative emotions, it can create physical tension and stress in your body. Letting go can help us release that tension and promote relaxation, which can have positive effects on your overall health. Chronically bad thinking can ultimately lead to a chronically bad body.

Next, we will explore some key areas we will focus on to help you better understand the benefits of letting go without giving up. You will notice there are several sections that show a reoccurring theme around increased mental and emotional health, increased self-awareness, and increased physical health, to name a few. It's important to recognize that there are several aspects to achieving these goals, as outlined further. The upcoming chapters in part 2 will then explore details on how to apply the techniques in letting go.

Introduction

Life is full of ups and downs, and we all experience times when we feel stuck or weighed down by the past. It can be hard to move forward when we're holding on to things that no longer serve us. Whether it's a past relationship, bitterness, or a habit that's no longer healthy, letting go can be a powerful tool for growth and transformation.

This also includes future experiences or the anticipation of something you desire – something you want. This, too, can inhibit your current state of well-being. Furthermore, your present world may be preventing you from living the full life you deserve. Past, present, and future are all aspects that motivate your positive and negative experiences. It is up to you to decide which road you choose to travel. You have the control within you, but not the control you may think. Part of the controlling factor is, in some cases, letting go of trying to own the situation – trying to change it.

Letting go is the act of releasing attachment to something that no longer serves you, whether it stems from the past, present, or future. It means accepting what is instead of trying to control or change it. It's not about giving up or resigning yourself to a situation but rather about finding the strength to move forward and create positive change in your life.

Stuff happens. You might have lost your job. You might have lost a loved one. Or you have just won the lottery. Or perhaps you made a new friend. Whether it's good or bad, it's up to you to choose how to deal with it. In some respects, one person's good is another's bad. Or vice versa, for that matter. Life is a give-and-take journey filled with ups and downs, ins and outs, the good and bad. The only thing you can ultimately control is your attitude and perspective on life. Your greatest initiative should be getting your heart, mind, and soul aligned.

There's also the situation where you get stuck in a rut. SSDD – Same Stuff Different Day. You have a feeling there's more to life than where you're at. Yet you fear the change. That's okay – most people like things to be ordinary and predictable. There's a sense of comfort in that. But is that what you're here for? Do you want to become a mundane robot going about your typical way in your typical life at your typical job? Where is the fun in that?

On the other hand, one must not go off the deep end, always trying to change one's life. The hard question is to know when to switch gears – when change is good and when change is bad.

The answer is simple yet complex. First, you must understand what is good in the moment versus bad. And the only way to do that is to live in the moment. The here and now.

Don't get me wrong – being average and boring can be just fine. Just as long as you're happy with it. And there's the key word – happiness. When you let go, you're really trying to become happier and remove suffering.

Living in the 'now' can be one of the most critical components for one to achieve in life. Nowness is an alignment between the heart, mind, and soul. Together they can help you understand best when to let go without giving up.

Learning to let go is a process that takes time and practice. But the benefits are many: improved mental and emotional health, reduced stress and anxiety, better relationships, and a greater sense of inner peace. Letting go can help us live more fully in the present moment and create space for new opportunities and experiences.

One of the most important aspects of letting go is to understand that it is not giving up. You should not forget the negative things you cling to, but you can spend time and effort to forgive them. When you give up on something, you are not trying to bury the memory. On the contrary, part of the process is in accepting what has happened or what you are thinking. Let them come and go as they please, but do not hold on to them, or else you will become trapped and entangled with attachment.

This book is a guide to the art of letting go and will explore what "letting go" means, why it's important, and how to do it in practical terms. We'll look at common obstacles to letting go and techniques for overcoming them. We'll explore specific situations where letting go can be particularly challenging, such as past relationships, negative self-talk, and material possessions.

Along the way, you may discover a more positive understanding of compassion, empathy, self-confidence, and the realization that you are not alone. Letting go is a detachment of that to which you are attached. But be careful – you may just get attached to detachment. It's a slippery slope that must be done through careful effort and practice. But the ultimate goal, once you arrive, is to alleviate your suffering through the practice of effortlessly letting go.

Whether you're looking to make a big change in your life or simply seeking greater peace and clarity, the practice of letting go can help. By releasing attachment to what no longer benefits us, you can create space for a new world of growth and possibility.

We'll explore a range of techniques for letting go without giving up, including mindfulness meditation, cognitive-behavioral techniques, journaling, and visualization exercises, to name a few. We'll look at the benefits of each technique and how they can be applied in different situations.

It's important to note that letting go and living in the moment is not a one-time event but an ongoing process. Even when you've successfully let go of something, you may find yourself struggling again in the future, still haunted by the past. That's why this book is designed to be a practical guide that you can return to again and again as you navigate the ups and downs of life.

As we delve into the topic of letting go, it's also important to recognize that it can be a difficult and emotional journey too. We may be holding onto things that have deep meaning for us or that we've invested a lot of time and energy into. Letting go can also be a grieving process as we say goodbye to people, places, and things we've held onto for a long time.

But the good news is that you don't have to go through this journey alone. Throughout this book, we'll offer practical tips and exercises to help you let go, as well as encouragement and support. And remember, the journey of letting go is ultimately a journey toward greater freedom, clarity, joy, and, most of all, the pursuit of happiness.

You will notice throughout the chapters a reoccurring theme. Numerous topics and discussions correlate to helping you with your negative emotional or physical patterns. Mental clarity, sleep, stress, anxiety, etc., all overlap to some extent. That said, it's important to reiterate the value of these topics for you to enjoy greater awareness and positive life experiences. Hopefully, by this book's end, many positive patterns will be engrained in your vibrant new world of love, joy, and happiness.

So, let's begin this journey together and discover the power of letting go without giving up.

CHAPTER 2 - IMPROVED MENTAL AND EMOTIONAL HEALTH

When we're holding onto something, it can create stress, anxiety, and other negative emotions. Letting go without giving up can help us release that tension and find greater peace.

Here are a few specific ways that letting go can improve our mental and emotional health.

Reduced Rumination

Have you ever found yourself in a situation where you just couldn't stop thinking about something that happened in the past? Maybe it was an argument with a loved one or a mistake you made at work. Whatever it was, you couldn't shake it from your mind.

When we hold onto something like that, it can create a cycle of rumination - where we constantly replay the event in our heads, trying to make sense of it or figure out what we could have done differently. This can lead to feelings of anxiety, depression, and even insomnia. Processing the thought or memory is good, provided you don't let it consume your life.

But when we learn to let go, we break that cycle. We're able to accept what happened and move on rather than getting stuck in a never-ending loop of negative thoughts. This can reduce rumination and give us greater peace of mind.

This does not mean you are trying to forget what has happened. Rather you process the thought, letting it come in and out of your mind, reminding yourself that while something negative happened in the past, it should not dictate your future. All it means is that you did something bad, but it is up to you how you utilize the experience going forward. It does not mean you are a bad person here and now.

Here are some key advantages of reduced rumination in terms of enhancing mental and emotional health, along with the associated benefits of letting go:

Lower stress and anxiety levels: Reduced rumination can decrease stress and anxiety levels, as individuals spend less time dwelling on negative thoughts and experiences. Letting go of unproductive worries and embracing acceptance can further promote a more balanced emotional state, thereby reducing the stress and anxiety in our life.

Improved mood and emotional well-being: Decreasing

rumination can help to improve mood and overall emotional well-being, as individuals experience fewer negative emotions and thoughts. Letting go of past hurts and disappointments can foster a more positive outlook, a stronger sense of inner peace, and a more robust outlook on life.

Enhanced mental clarity and focus: Reduced rumination can lead to greater mental clarity and focus, as individuals are less preoccupied with repetitive thoughts. Letting go of distractions and unhelpful thought patterns can further sharpen mental clarity and promote better decision-making. It also fills your life with more energy to get things done.

Better problem-solving abilities: Lower levels of rumination can contribute to improved problem-solving abilities, as individuals can approach challenges with a clearer and more objective mindset. Letting go of the need to overanalyze situations can support more effective problem-solving strategies. Analysis of your thoughts and past experiences is important, provided it does not hinder a positive outlook on life.

Increased resilience and coping skills: Getting rid of rumination can enhance an individual's resilience and ability to cope with stress and adversity. Letting go of unhelpful coping mechanisms and adopting healthier strategies can further support the ability to manage stress and emotional challenges. The increased resilience will also help with improved energy levels.

Greater self-awareness and personal growth: Reduced rumination can promote greater self-awareness and personal growth, as individuals can better understand their emotions and actions or reactions. Letting go of self-judgment and embracing self-compassion can foster a more authentic and compassionate relationship with oneself and those around you.

Enhanced interpersonal relationships: Decreasing rumination can lead to improved interpersonal relationships, as individuals are better able to engage in the present moment and communicate more effectively with others. Letting go of unresolved conflicts and resentments can further support healthier and more satisfying connections with others. Ruminating over past thoughts will only block your engagement with others.

Improved sleep quality: Reduced rumination can contribute to better sleep quality, as individuals spend less time dwelling on concerns and negative thoughts before bedtime. Letting go of racing thoughts and worries can promote a night of more restful and rejuvenating sleep. If anything, let the thoughts come and go – they are something you can think through in the morning if need be.

Increased sense of control and well-being: By reducing rumination, individuals can gain a greater sense of control over their thoughts and emotions, empowering them to manage their mental and emotional health more effectively. Letting go of the need for constant control and embracing the present moment can foster a more balanced and peaceful state of mind. Don't let control of the negative thoughts control of you.

Prevention of mental health issues: Lower levels of rumination can help prevent or alleviate mental health issues, such as depression and anxiety, by reducing the persistence of negative thought patterns. Letting go of ruminative thinking and adopting healthier cognitive strategies can support overall mental and emotional health. You must try to stop the negative thoughts from taking over your daily life.

By incorporating the practice of letting go and focusing on reducing rumination, individuals can experience numerous benefits for their mental and emotional health, promoting greater well-being, resilience, and personal growth. Next, we will get into more discussion about stress and anxiety levels.

Lower Stress and Anxiety Levels

Lowering stress and anxiety levels can have numerous benefits for improving mental and emotional health and physical health. When individuals can manage their stress and anxiety effectively, they are better able to cope with daily challenges, maintain positive relationships, and maintain a positive outlook on life. Incorporating the concept of letting go can further enhance these benefits by releasing attachment to old patterns of negative thinking and behaviors and embracing new ways of relaxation, mindfulness, and positivity. You will begin to find more joy in your life.

Some key advantages of lower stress and anxiety levels in promoting mental and emotional health include improved mood and emotional well-being, decision-making, cognitive function, and overall mental health. By letting go of attachment to old patterns of stress and worry, individuals can lower their stress and anxiety levels, leading to these benefits and a greater sense of well-being.

By incorporating the practice of letting go without giving up and focusing on lowering stress and anxiety levels, individuals can experience numerous benefits for promoting mental and emotional health, fostering personal growth and self-awareness, and fostering a sense of inner peace and well-being.

Here are some key advantages of lower stress and anxiety levels in terms of improving mental and emotional health, along with the associated benefits of letting go:

Improved mood: Lower stress and anxiety levels can lead to improved mood, as individuals are better able to experience positive emotions and find joy in their daily lives. Letting go of attachment to old patterns of negative thinking and embracing new ways of relaxation and positivity can promote improved mood and emotional well-being. In short, you just simply feel better.

Improved cognitive function: Lower stress and anxiety levels can also contribute to improved cognitive function, as individuals are better able to focus, think clearly, and make sound decisions in the present moment. Letting go of attachment to old patterns of stress and worry and embracing new ways of relaxation and mindfulness can promote improved cognitive function and mental clarity.

Improved sleep: Lower stress and anxiety levels can also contribute to improved sleep, as individuals are better able to relax and get the rest they need. Letting go of attachment to old patterns of stress and worry and embracing new ways of relaxation and self-care can promote improved sleep and overall well-being. Ideally, you should sleep seven to eight hours each night on average. Lowering the stress in your life will easily help with this.

Enhanced relationships: Lower stress and anxiety levels can also contribute to enhanced relationships, as individuals are better able to communicate effectively, manage conflict, and express empathy. Letting go of attachment to old conflict and negativity patterns and embracing new relaxation and positive communication can promote improved relationships and greater emotional connection.

Improved overall mental health: Lower stress and anxiety levels can contribute to improved overall mental health, as individuals are better able to manage their emotions, cope with stress, and maintain a positive outlook. Letting go of attachment to old ways of negative thinking and embracing new patterns of relaxation, mindfulness, and positivity can promote improved mental health and well-being.

By incorporating the practice of letting go and focusing on lower stress and anxiety levels, individuals can experience numerous benefits for improving mental and emotional health, promoting personal growth and self-awareness, and fostering a sense of inner peace and well-being. The first step is to recognize unwanted stress and anxiety, then apply practical techniques that we will discuss later in this book.

Improved Mood and
Emotional Well-Being

An improved mood and emotional well-being can improve mental and emotional health while living in the present moment. When individuals can experience positive emotions and manage negative emotions effectively, they are better able to cope with stress, maintain positive relationships, and make sound decisions. Incorporating the concept of letting go without giving up can further enhance these benefits by releasing attachment to old ways of thinking or behaving that is bad.

Some key advantages of improved mood and emotional well-being in terms of promoting mental and emotional health include reduced risk of depression, improved self-esteem, improved relationships, improved cognitive function, and improved overall mental health. By letting go of attachment to old patterns of negative thinking and behaviors, individuals can improve their mood and emotional well-being, leading to these benefits, a greater sense of well-being, and a more positive attitude toward life.

By practicing the art of letting go and focusing on improving mood and emotional well-being, individuals can experience numerous benefits for promoting better health, fostering personal growth and self-awareness, and fostering a sense of inner peace and well-being.

Here are some key advantages of improved mood and emotional well-being in terms of promoting mental and emotional health, along with the associated benefits of letting go:

Reduced risk of depression: Improved mood and emotional well-being can lead to a reduced risk of depression, as individuals are better able to experience positive emotions and find joy in their daily lives. Letting go of attachment to old patterns of negative thinking and replacing them with new options of relaxation and positivity can alleviate the cycle of chronic depression. Reducing your emotional barriers in life will help break free of bad thoughts.

Improved self-esteem: Improved mood and emotional well-being can also give way to improved self-esteem, as individuals are better able to appreciate their own worth and value. Letting go of attachment to negative self-talk and embracing new ways of self-care and positivity can promote enhanced self-esteem and greater self-worth.

Improved relationships: Improved mood and emotional well-being can also contribute to enhanced relationships, as individuals are better able to communicate effectively, manage conflict, and express empathy. Letting go of attachment to repeating patterns of conflict and negativity can help provide new pathways to relaxation and positive communication and, in turn, can promote improved relationships and greater emotional connection. After all, we are social creatures in general, and being in a positive frame of mind will allow engaging with others more effectively.

Improved cognitive function: Improved mood and emotional well-being can also aid in improved cognitive function, as individuals are better able to focus, think clearly, and make correct decisions in the moment. Letting go of attachment to inappropriate stress and worry can lead to better ways of relaxation and mindfulness and, in turn, promotes improved cognitive function and mental clarity.

Improved overall mental health: Improved mood and emotional well-being can contribute to improved overall mental health, as individuals are better able to manage their emotions, cope with stress, and maintain a positive outlook. Letting go of attachment to old patterns of negative thinking and embracing new ways of relaxation, mindfulness, and positivity can promote improved mental health and overall well-being.

By incorporating the practice of letting go and focusing on improving mood and emotional well-being, individuals can experience numerous benefits for promoting mental and emotional health, fostering personal growth and self-awareness, and fostering a sense of inner peace and well-being. The key is to find that positive inner foundation from which to live. This allows you to think more clearly and focus on what is needed in the moment – which we will be discussing next.

Enhanced Mental Clarity and Focus

Enhanced mental clarity and focus can have numerous benefits for improving mental and emotional health. When individuals can clear their minds and focus their attention more effectively, they are better able to manage their emotions, make decisions, and engage in positive relationships with others. Incorporating the concept of letting go can further enhance these benefits by releasing attachment to your old ways of thinking. This will allow you to fully embrace new opportunities for relaxation, mindfulness, and positivity.

Some key advantages of enhanced mental clarity and focus in terms of promoting mental and emotional health include improved decision-making, reduced risk of anxiety, improved productivity, improved overall mental health, and enhanced relationships.

With the practice of letting go and focusing on enhancing mental clarity and focus, you can experience numerous benefits for promoting mental and emotional health, fostering personal growth and self-awareness, and fostering a sense of inner peace and well-being.

Here are some key advantages of enhanced mental clarity and focus in terms of promoting mental and emotional health, along with the associated benefits of letting go:

Improved decision-making: Enhanced mental clarity and focus can lead to improved decision-making, as individuals can better analyze situations in the moment or future plans and weigh the pros and cons of different options. Removing the attachment through letting go of stress and worry will allow you to embrace relaxation and mindfulness techniques to promote enhanced mental clarity and focus, thereby improving decision-making skills. Much of what we do stems from thinking clearly. If you can't think right, you are thinking wrong.

Reduced risk of anxiety: Enhanced mental clarity and focus can also contribute to reduced risk of anxiety, as individuals are better able to manage their thoughts and emotions. Being anxious for no reason will never let you be free. Remove the attachment of these old patterns of anxiety. This will free your mind to focus on more important thoughts and plans.

Improved productivity: Enhanced mental clarity and focus can also influence improved productivity, as individuals are better able to stay focused on tasks and complete them efficiently. Letting go of distractions will detach you from the bad execution of actions or thoughts. You will find yourself doing more for yourself as well as those around you.

Improved overall mental health: Enhanced mental clarity and focus can also contribute to improved overall mental health, as individuals are better able to manage their emotions and maintain a positive outlook. You will be in a better state of mind to embrace a more comfortable world of relaxation, mindfulness, and positivity. Take time to calm down in the moment and remember you have value to contribute to yourself as well as those around you.

Improved relationships: Improving your relationships can also help for mental clarity and focus. You will be able to communicate effectively better and manage current conflicts. Letting go of attachment to these ugly patterns of negative thinking will only enhance the relationships you are involved with. Thinking clearly is key.

By including the practice of self-awareness and focusing on enhancing mental clarity and focus, individuals can experience many benefits for promoting mental and emotional health, fostering personal growth and self-awareness, and fostering a sense of inner peace and well-being. This, in turn, promotes mindfulness and less suffering. Your mind will be less cluttered with negative thoughts so that you can focus on the rewards of positive thinking.

Better Problem-Solving Abilities

Having better problem-solving abilities can have countless benefits for improving mental and emotional health. When individuals can analyze situations and come up with effective solutions, they are better able to cope with challenges and make sound decisions. Incorporating the concept of letting go can further enhance these benefits by releasing attachment to bed patterns of useless problem-solving skills.

When solving problems, you must 'think outside the box' sometimes. Put yourself in someone else's shoes and utilize critical thinking. Just don't overthink the problem. It can be difficult to understand when to think and when to act, and how much to think or act. But with a balanced level of mental and emotional well-being, you can find the appropriate levels to think and act from to solve problems around you.

Some key advantages of having better problem-solving abilities in promoting mental and emotional health include reduced stress and anxiety, improved decision-making, relationships, self-esteem, and overall mental health. All of which we have touched on previously. Yet all of these are critical to better problem-solving in the moment.

Letting go and focusing on improving problem-solving abilities will help you promote mental and emotional health, foster personal growth and self-awareness, and foster a sense of inner peace and well-being. It will feel good to be in the now and find yourself effortlessly solving problems and situations you never thought you could do. With enough practice, it will feel like intuition where you're not thinking.

Here are some benefits of better problem-solving abilities as it pertains to improved mental and emotional health, including how the concept of letting go can enhance these benefits:

Reduced stress and anxiety: By solving problems

effectively, individuals can reduce their stress and anxiety levels related to the challenge at hand. Letting go of attachment to negative thinking skills and emotions can further reduce stress and anxiety. They kind of go together, where you won't be able to solve problems well if you're always anxious and stressed out.

Improved decision-making: Good problem-solving abilities can lead to improved decision-making in all areas of life, including personal and professional relationships. You may find yourself trying to make decisions about getting married, buying a new house, or finding a new job. By chilling out and relaxing, you can make better decisions. Letting go in the moment can help with this and help you make more informed decisions based on current circumstances.

Improved relationships: When you can effectively solve problems, you can communicate your needs and desires more clearly and resolve conflicts in a constructive manner. You are less likely to make inappropriate decisions with others. You can also express yourself more clearly, aligning more positively with your true desire and expectations. Being open and honest will also help in a relationship. Working together on the problems you are trying to solve will be that much easier when you're in the right frame of mind by letting go.

Improved self-esteem: Successfully solving problems can boost self-confidence and self-esteem. Letting go of attachment to negative self-talk and self-doubt can further improve self-esteem and promote a positive self-image. The more you practice letting go while problem-solving, the more successful you will be in how you perceive yourself. You will find yourself present with problems yet easily understand what the solution should be. In turn, this promotes a greater send of self-esteem.

Improved overall mental health: Developing strong problem-solving skills can lead to greater control over one's life, which can positively impact overall mental health. Practicing letting go will help you mentally feel better, allowing you to continue work from a state of well-being and inner peace, further enriching your abilities to solve problems.

In summary, the benefits of better problem-solving abilities in terms of improving mental and emotional health include reduced stress and anxiety, improved decision-making, improved relationships, improved self-esteem, and improved overall mental health.

By practicing the art of letting go without giving up, you can enhance these benefits by releasing attachment to negative thoughts and behaviors and embracing positivity and mindfulness. With enough practice, you will find yourself solving problems without thinking and later ponder how you can be so effective without thinking.

Increased Self-Awareness

Letting go can be a challenging process requiring us to look hard at ourselves and our emotions. It forces us to confront the thoughts and beliefs holding us back and question whether they're positively serving us.

Through this process, we develop greater self-awareness and understanding of ourselves. We start to see our patterns of behavior and thought more clearly, and we begin to recognize the ways in which they may be limiting us. This increased self-awareness can be incredibly empowering, as it allows us to make positive changes in our lives and break free from old patterns.

Spending time 'listening' to your thoughts is critical. For the most part, practicing mindfulness helps you 'watch' the thoughts come and go, detaching you from them and letting them go, thereby removing the attachment to them.

In a way, letting go can be seen as an act of self-care - by taking the time to examine our emotions and beliefs, we're investing in our own growth and greater well-being. We will be able to live our lives the way we are supposed to – with love, compassion, and joy.

The hard part is understanding who the thinker is. If you are the one thinking and watching the thoughts, who is the one watching? This begins to dive into the realm of spirituality or the idea that you are more than just a bag of bones. Even if you don't believe in spirituality, there is a level of consciousness most people never realize. They can end up living as zombies on parade.

Here are some key advantages of greater self-awareness in terms of enhancing mental and emotional health, along with the associated benefits of letting go:

Improved emotional regulation: Increased self-awareness can lead to better emotional regulation as individuals become more attuned to their emotions and reactions. They don't fly off the handle at a moment's notice. Letting go of judgment and embracing self-compassion can further promote a balanced emotional state and healthier responses to stressors.

Enhanced resilience and coping skills: Greater self-awareness can improve resilience and the ability to cope with stress and adversity. Like it or not, stress will always be there. The key is in how you deal with it. Letting go of unhelpful coping mechanisms such as over-eating or even over-exercising can inhibit your life. Adopting healthier strategies can support the ability to manage emotional challenges more effectively and develop better ways to deal with stress.

Greater self-compassion and self-acceptance: As individuals become more self-aware, they can develop a deeper understanding of their strengths and weaknesses, fostering greater self-compassion and self-acceptance. You find yourself accepting who you are and what you do more easily. You understand that you are more than just your thoughts and actions. There is a sense of inner peace from which you can reflect on the more important values in life. Letting go of unrealistic expectations and self-criticism can further enhance self-compassion and overall emotional well-being.

Healthier interpersonal relationships: Increased self-awareness can lead to improved interpersonal relationships, as individuals are better able to communicate their needs, boundaries, and emotions effectively. Through self-awareness, you can better manage the world around you and those whom you interact with. You will also provide a better world for them. Letting go of unresolved conflicts and resentments can support healthier and more satisfying connections with others.

Better decision-making and problem-solving: Greater self-awareness can contribute to better decision-making and problem-solving abilities, as individuals can approach challenges with a clearer understanding of their values, priorities, and emotions. Being more self-aware allows you to think more clearly and make better decisions in the moment. Letting go of the need to overanalyze situations can further promote effective problem-solving strategies. Don't overthink things that don't need too much thought.

Enhanced personal growth and self-improvement: Increased self-awareness can lead to greater personal growth and self-improvement, as individuals can identify areas for growth and implement changes more effectively. You are freer to adapt to the changes around you through being more self-aware. You will find yourself growing more positive as you modify the way you are thinking and acting. Letting go of past failures and focusing on progress can support a growth mindset and continued personal development.

Improved mental health: Greater self-awareness can help prevent or alleviate mental health issues, such as depression and anxiety, by fostering healthier emotional regulation and coping strategies. It may not make sense, but you must listen to your mind. Detach from the everyday mindless thinking and think about the person doing the thinking. As thoughts come and go, be aware of them, but don't overreact. Letting go of negative thought patterns and embracing healthier cognitive strategies can further support overall mental and emotional health.

Increased sense of control and well-being: By enhancing self-awareness, individuals can gain a greater sense of control over their thoughts and emotions, empowering them to manage their mental and emotional health more effectively. Be careful, however, as control may have gotten you in a bad place. Letting go does not mean the removal of control. Rather it's an internal reflection of the things that need to be controlled and the things that do not. Letting go of the need for constant control and embracing the present moment can foster a more balanced and peaceful state of mind.

Better stress management: Increased self-awareness can contribute to more effective stress management as individuals become better equipped to recognize and address their stressors. You may find yourself observing situations that are stressful yet not reacting negatively. Some stress is good for you, like if a gunman is coming toward you. Yet much of what we stress about is pointless. Understanding what to stress about and what not to is critical. Letting go of excessive worry and things you can't control is important, as well as adopting healthier coping mechanisms to provide further stress reduction.

Greater life satisfaction: As individuals become more self-aware and develop a deeper understanding of their emotions, needs, and values, they can experience greater life satisfaction and overall well-being. You will find yourself seeing the more positive side of life, and the negative situations don't seem to bother you as much. Life is full of things that come and go, yet you remain. Detach yourself from the bad thoughts, and your life will be that much better. Letting go of external validation and focusing on personal growth and fulfillment can further enhance life satisfaction.

Cultivating self-awareness is an ongoing process that involves reflection, self-examination, and openness to feedback. By enhancing self-awareness, individuals can improve various aspects of their lives, from personal growth and emotional well-being to relationship quality and professional success.

Improved Self-Esteem

Holding onto negative emotions, beliefs, or experiences can really weigh us down and damage our self-esteem. When we're constantly replaying negative events in our minds or dwelling on past mistakes, it can create feelings of shame, guilt, or inadequacy, thoughts that I am not worthy of this life.

However, when we learn to let go, we free ourselves from those negative perceptions and beliefs. We start to recognize that our mistakes or past experiences do not define us and that we have the power to create positive change in our lives. We are in control of what we choose to control. This can help us feel more confident and self-assured, leading to a stronger sense of self-esteem. Do not stay attached to what happened in the past. Don't forget all the experiences; just change your mind to embrace the thoughts in a positive way. This will eventually lead you to the path of forgiveness – not just for others but, more importantly, for yourself.

When we let go of negative beliefs and emotions, we create space for more positive thoughts and feelings to come in. After all, you can't stop thinking but can control what you think about. We begin to see ourselves in a more positive light, and we're able to recognize our own worth and value. This can be incredibly empowering and help us feel more confident and self-assured in all aspects of our lives. Everyone on this earth has a reason to be here. Embrace your uniqueness, expand on it, and share it with others by letting go and having greater self-esteem.

Here are some key advantages of greater self-esteem in terms of enhancing mental and emotional health, along with the associated benefits of letting go:

Enhanced emotional well-being: Improved self-esteem can contribute to better emotional well-being as individuals experience more positive emotions and a greater sense of self-worth. You will find your emotions become more stable with greater self-esteem. You tend not to worry as much about what others are thinking about you. You have created a better foundation from which to live life by rejecting unneeded self-criticism and embracing self-compassion.

Greater resilience and coping skills: Higher self-esteem can improve resilience and the ability to cope with stress and adversity. Even when things don't go your way, you have a level of confidence in yourself to work from. Bad things will come and go, but you can weather the storms with greater self-esteem. Your coping skills can be modified to provide a better environment. Letting go of unhelpful coping mechanisms and adopting healthier strategies can support the ability to manage emotional challenges more effectively.

Healthier interpersonal relationships: Improved self-esteem can lead to healthier interpersonal relationships, as individuals with high self-esteem are more likely to communicate their needs and boundaries effectively and engage in more satisfying connections with others. Many situations no longer bother you as you have a more solid foundation within yourself. Letting go of past disappointments and focusing on building positive relationships can further enhance interpersonal connections.

Better decision-making and problem-solving: Greater self-esteem can contribute to better decision-making and problem-solving abilities, as individuals with high self-esteem are more likely to trust their instincts and make choices that align with their values and priorities. The way in which you approach problems tends to be more comfortable for those with higher self-esteem. You understand you may not be able to solve all the problems in the world, but with greater confidence, you can apply yourself more effectively and resolve conflicts as best you can without creating self-doubt. Letting go of self-doubt and embracing self-confidence can further promote effective problem-solving strategies.

Increased motivation and goal achievement: Improved self-esteem can lead to increased motivation and goal achievement, as individuals with high self-esteem are more likely to pursue their goals and aspirations. You become freer to reach for the stars and less concerned about falling. While remembering your failures from the past, you can forgive yourself and move forward with planning your goals for the future. Self-esteem enhances your motivation to do more in life, not less. Letting go of past failures and focusing on progress can support a growth mindset and continued personal development.

Reduced risk of mental health issues: Greater self-esteem can help prevent or alleviate mental health issues, such as depression and anxiety, by fostering a more positive self-image and healthier coping strategies. Clearly, if you have serious mental health issues, you should reach out for help. Yet mild or temporary depression can be alleviated through increased self-esteem. Letting go of negative thought patterns and embracing healthier cognitive strategies can further support overall mental and emotional health.

Increased sense of control and well-being: By enhancing self-esteem, individuals can gain greater control over their thoughts and emotions, empowering them to manage their mental and emotional health more effectively. Greater self-esteem allows you to handle difficult situations with greater ease. You will find yourself not losing control as much but rather finding a better understanding of what you can control and what cannot. Letting go of the need for external validation and focusing on personal growth and fulfillment can foster a more balanced and peaceful state of mind.

Better stress management: Improved self-esteem can contribute to more effective stress management, as individuals with high self-esteem are better equipped to recognize and address their stressors. As mentioned previously, there will always be stress in your life. But with greater self-esteem, you can manage the stress that much better. Letting go of excessive worry and adopting healthier mental and emotional coping mechanisms through enhanced self-esteem can further promote stress reduction.

Greater life satisfaction: As individuals improve their self-esteem and develop a stronger sense of self-worth, they can experience greater life satisfaction and overall well-being. You can find yourself appreciating the simpler things in life with greater self-esteem. Don't sweat the small stuff – embrace it with love, compassion, and understanding. Letting go of comparisons to others and embracing one's unique strengths and qualities can further enhance life satisfaction.

Enhanced personal growth and self-improvement: Improved self-esteem can lead to greater personal growth and self-improvement, as individuals are more likely to invest in their own development and well-being. You may find yourself discovering new things to do or old things in a new light. Learn a better way of life through greater self-esteem. Letting go of limiting beliefs and embracing one's potential can support continued growth and self-discovery.

By concentrating on letting go and improving self-esteem, individuals can experience numerous mental and emotional health benefits, promoting greater well-being, resilience, and personal growth. Keep calm and grow. Find a better balance in life, starting with your internal mental and emotional self. If you are not centered, how do you expect the rest of the world to be centered?

Greater Emotional Resilience

When we can let go of things holding us back, it can help us build emotional resilience. We become better able to handle difficult situations and bounce back from setbacks because negative emotions do not weigh us down. Instead, we're able to stay focused on the present moment and the positive things in our lives. Emotional resilience prevents us from dwelling on the bad things of the past. This can give us a sense of inner strength and help us face challenges with more confidence and optimism.

With practice, letting go will allow you to let your thoughts come and go. You will not be so quick to respond to negative energy. When something bad confronts you, it's easy to fall into your negative patterns and beliefs immediately. But with a keen focus on your thoughts, you can expand your horizon and recognize compassion and empathy for the current situation.

It's not that you have removed your emotions. Rather you have fortified them in a more positive way. You can choose how to react to your environment, including your thoughts. This, in turn, provides you with emotional resilience. As stated previously, you position yourself to choose what you control in your life.

Here are some key advantages of increased emotional resilience in terms of enhancing mental and emotional health, along with the associated benefits of letting go:

Improved stress management: Emotional resilience can contribute to better stress management, as individuals with greater resilience are better equipped to handle stressors and adapt to change. Change can be a good thing if you have the right attitude. While it can create stress in dealing with the unknown, it can also be enlightening to a new way of life. Managing stress in life through letting go is critical to greater well-being. Observe what stresses you, question its value, then deal with it. Letting go of excessive worry can further promote stress reduction.

Enhanced emotional well-being: Increased emotional resilience can lead to better emotional well-being, as individuals are more capable of managing negative emotions and recovering from setbacks. Let the situations come and go, along with your thoughts. Take time, when possible, to listen to your emotions and act upon them accordingly. Letting go of self-criticism and embracing self-compassion can further promote emotional balance and overall well-being.

Greater coping skills: Emotional resilience is associated with improved coping skills, as resilient individuals can develop and utilize healthier strategies for managing stress and adversity. Don't just reach for a snack when you're bored. Ask yourself why you are bored. Or don't run away from a problem because you hate conflict. That said, running away is just fine if imminent danger exists. The key is to rethink your coping skills before you need them – be more proactive with your emotional and mental health. Letting go of unhelpful coping mechanisms and adopting more effective strategies can support the ability to manage emotional challenges more effectively.

Better interpersonal relationships: Greater emotional resilience can lead to healthier interpersonal relationships, as individuals with high resilience are more likely to communicate effectively and navigate conflicts with others. By letting go, you will find yourself in a more stable emotional environment in which to work. You tend not to get 'crazy' because your emotions are in check. And the people around you will notice. Letting go of past disappointments and focusing on building positive relationships can further enhance interpersonal connections.

Increased motivation and goal achievement: Improved emotional resilience can contribute to increased motivation and goal achievement, as individuals with high resilience are more likely to persevere in the face of obstacles and setbacks. By letting go, you will find yourself in a more peaceful setting and find more motivation to do things in life. Your goals will be better aligned with more positive achievements. Letting go of past failures and focusing on progress can support a growth mindset and continued personal development.

Reduced risk of mental health issues: Greater emotional resilience can help prevent or alleviate mental health issues, such as depression and anxiety, by fostering healthier emotional regulation and coping strategies. Not being centered and balanced with your emotional and mental health will only send you off in the wrong direction. It's okay to be instinctive, provided your instincts are correct. By letting go and having greater emotional resilience, your state of mind can remove negative thought patterns and embrace healthier cognitive strategies.

Enhanced self-esteem and self-confidence: Emotional resilience can contribute to improved self-esteem and self-confidence, as resilient individuals develop a stronger sense of self-worth and trust in their abilities. Everything you do stems from a balanced emotional state. Even when things go wrong, you realize it's okay. You know through greater self-esteem and self-confidence that you are worthy of the situation – good or bad. Letting go of self-doubt and embracing self-confidence can further promote personal growth and well-being.

Greater life satisfaction: As individuals develop greater emotional resilience, they can experience increased life satisfaction and overall well-being due to their ability to navigate challenges and recover from setbacks more effectively. Whether good things or bad things happen to you, with enhanced emotional resilience, you can work through all of it. You no longer focus on the negative issues in your life. Letting go of comparisons to others and embracing one's unique strengths and qualities can further enhance life satisfaction.

Increased adaptability and flexibility: Emotional resilience is associated with increased adaptability and flexibility, as resilient individuals can better adjust to changes and new situations. You don't feel so trapped in past feelings and beliefs. Things don't have to be done in the same way as before. Think differently. Think better. Through emotional resilience, you can find a better place from which to think and act. Letting go of the need for constant control and embracing the present moment can foster a more balanced and peaceful state of mind.

Enhanced personal growth and self-improvement: Greater emotional resilience can lead to enhanced personal growth and self-improvement, as individuals are more likely to learn from challenges and setbacks and use these experiences to foster personal development. By letting your thoughts come and go, you can begin to grow. The negative thoughts of the past will not slow you down. They are just thoughts. Through this process, you can improve upon the world you live in in a more positive way. You feel better about yourself, challenge yourself to do more, and get better at what you do. Letting go of limiting beliefs and embracing one's potential can support continued growth and self-discovery.

By incorporating the practice of letting go and focusing on developing greater emotional resilience, individuals can experience numerous benefits for their mental and emotional health, promoting greater well-being, resilience, and personal growth. Dare to be different, unique, and special, but you will only be truly successful if your emotional resilience is in place.

CHAPTER 3 -
REDUCED STRESS
AND ANXIETY

Holding onto negative emotions like anger, resentment, or regret can create a constant undercurrent of stress and anxiety in our lives. It can make us feel like we're carrying a heavy burden on our shoulders. Contrary to what you may think, the weight of the world is not on your shoulders. That said, the weight of *your* world is. How will you address this? There are things you can control and things you cannot. Understanding that is critical to reducing stress and anxiety.

However, when we learn to let go of those emotions and feelings, we can experience greater peace and relief. Keep in mind that we are not letting go of the memories – just the negative emotions associated with them. Emotions are key to being human but holding onto negative ones is not productive. By releasing that tension and stress, we're able to focus more on the positive aspects of our lives, which can reduce feelings of anxiety and improve our overall life. That weight on your shoulder becomes lighter. It's still there, just not as heavy.

Below are a few benefits of removing stress and anxiety in your life by letting go. While the topics are like previous discussions, it's important to dig a little deeper into the aspects from a stress and anxiety perspective.

Improved Sleep

Holding onto something can create a constant undercurrent of stress and anxiety, making it difficult to relax and fall asleep at night. Too many rampant thoughts are swirling around in your head. The negative emotions can keep our minds racing and prevent us from getting a restful night's sleep. Letting go can help us release that tension and find greater peace, improving our sleep. When we're able to let go of our worries and concerns, we can create a calmer and more peaceful state of mind, which is conducive to better sleep.

Spending time before bed on worrisome thoughts will not help you enjoy your slumber. Instead, try to review what's bothering you earlier in the day. And don't force the thoughts to go away. Blocking them will only delay the inevitable. Let them come in and go out like the waves in the ocean.

Here are some key advantages of better sleep in terms of reducing stress and anxiety, along with the associated benefits of letting go:

Enhanced emotional regulation: Improved sleep can contribute to better emotional regulation, as adequate rest allows the brain to process emotions more effectively. Many people wonder why they must sleep in the first place. Others are bothered by wasting precious time with sleep rather than staying awake to do more things. Like it or not, your brain and body need time to reset. Some would argue that your spirit or consciousness needs this time too. Sleep is also needed to rebalance your emotional state. Letting go of worries and adopting relaxation techniques before bedtime can further promote emotional balance and well-being.

Reduced stress hormone levels: Better sleep can help lower stress hormone levels, such as cortisol, which can reduce the overall stress response. It's a natural process when having a good night's sleep to decrease cortisol and allow your body to heal. Doing so helps keep your hormone levels in check while awake. Letting go of the day's stressors and engaging in calming activities before sleep can further support healthy hormone levels.

Increased mental clarity and focus: Improved sleep can lead to increased mental clarity and focus, as adequate rest helps the brain to function more efficiently. Your brain is still processing things while you're snoring away. Think of it like a computer that is doing diagnostics to improve performance. Without sleep, mental clarity and focus during the day could slow down and inhibit your ability to process situations and activities. Letting go of ruminative thoughts and embracing mindfulness practices can promote better sleep and improved cognitive functioning.

Enhanced immune system function: Better sleep can contribute to a stronger immune system, which can help the body better cope with stress and anxiety. While everyone understands it's important to have a healthy immune system, most people don't take the time to achieve it. This includes finding enough time to sleep. Just like the mind needs time while you sleep to reset, so does your body. Without sleep, your mind and body will constantly be building up more stress and anxiety. Letting go of unhealthy habits and adopting a balanced sleep schedule can further support immune health.

Improved mood and overall well-being: Adequate sleep can help improve mood and overall well-being, as it allows the body and mind to recharge and rejuvenate. For those who have spent a late-night partying or playing video games, then having to get up early for work, you've probably noticed how you wake up in a lousy mood and don't feel right. Sure, doing this occasionally can be exciting, but not something you want to engage with on a daily basis. On average, getting a good night's sleep is critical to your mood and well-being.

Greater resilience and coping skills: Improved sleep can lead to greater resilience and the ability to cope with stress and adversity more effectively. Have you ever woken up in the morning after only getting a couple of hours of sleep and can't think straight? Brain fog is still lingering as you shower and head to work, further lingering throughout the morning. You find it impossible to deal with any level of stress and are easy to blow up in even the simplest of situations. Yet when you get a decent amount of sleep, you're ready to take on the day. Problems that arise are more easily handled. Getting enough sleep allows you to be more resilient throughout the day, and your ability to cope with situations is that much easier.

Reduced anxiety symptoms: Getting better sleep can help alleviate anxiety symptoms, as sleep disturbances are often linked to increased anxiety levels. Being fully rested allows you to start the day right with less anxiety. Or if stress comes about, you can handle it more effectively. Letting go of excessive worry and incorporating relaxation techniques can promote a more restful and rejuvenating sleep experience.

Increased energy and vitality: Adequate sleep can contribute to increased energy and vitality, allowing individuals to manage stress and anxiety during the day better. A happy mind is a happy body. It can go both ways, but good sleep patterns can cover both. In doing so, your energy levels are increased, and you can deal with the stress and anxiety that shows up during the day. Letting go of sleep-disrupting habits and embracing a consistent sleep routine can further support overall energy levels.

Better decision-making and problem-solving: Improved sleep can enhance decision-making and problem-solving abilities, as the brain is better able to process information and think critically. As mentioned before, not getting enough sleep tends to give you brain fog that could last throughout the day. Poor choices may raise critical problems at home or at work, leading to a negative spiral of doom. Letting go of stress and anxiety through better sleep habits will provide a more positive environment to make correct decisions about the problems at hand.

Greater life satisfaction: As individuals experience better sleep and reduced stress and anxiety levels, they can experience greater life satisfaction and overall well-being. You just feel naturally better. Situations and activities tend to be more effortless. You find yourself with a more positive attitude toward life when you get enough sleep. Letting go of external stressors that inhibit your sleep and focusing on personal growth and self-care can further enhance life satisfaction.

Prioritizing good sleep hygiene, including maintaining a consistent sleep schedule, creating a relaxing bedtime routine, and ensuring a comfortable sleep environment, can lead to improved sleep quality and provide numerous benefits for the removal of stress and anxiety in your life. Of course, it's just one of many aspects of living life to its fullest. Next, we'll dive into more details about problem-solving.

Better Decision-Making and Problem-Solving

Better decision-making and problem-solving skills can have numerous benefits for reducing stress and anxiety, and incorporating the concept of letting go can further enhance these benefits. There's no greater cure to keen problem-solving than having your mind and body in the right place. Reducing the amount of stress in your life can only help in the equation. As mentioned before, stress in your life is not going away. But you can choose how you deal with it. Understanding when to be anxious and when not to is critical. Furthermore, making decisions and solving problems successfully can be most effective when your life is centered and balanced.

Let's explore some key advantages of improved decision-making and problem-solving in terms of reducing stress and anxiety, along with the associated benefits of letting go:

Increased sense of control: Better decision-making and problem-solving skills can contribute to increased control over life events and situations, reducing stress and anxiety. Being in the right state of mind allows you to feel in control of situations. That said, there will always be things out of your control. Yet, if the stress and anxiety in your life are lowered, you can better understand what you can and cannot control. Letting go of the need for constant control and embracing flexibility can further support a balanced mindset and emotional well-being.

Greater confidence in facing challenges: Improved decision-making and problem-solving abilities can help individuals feel more confident in facing challenges and navigating obstacles, reducing stress and anxiety associated with uncertain situations. Most people have a fear of the unknown and don't like change. By removing some of the stress in your life, you can address the challenges you face in a more positive way. You can feel more confident in facing the unknown by understanding and embracing your strengths and weaknesses. Letting go of self-doubt and embracing self-confidence can enhance personal growth and resilience.

Enhanced adaptability and flexibility: Good decision-making and problem-solving skills can promote adaptability and flexibility, as individuals are better equipped to adjust to changes and new circumstances. You no longer are holding tightly to the memories and experiences of the past. Rather, you open yourself up to being challenged by the situations that unfold, and through reduced stress, allow yourself to be flexible and adaptable. Letting go of rigid thinking patterns and embracing a more open-minded approach can further support adaptability and stress reduction.

Improved time management and prioritization: Effective decision-making and problem-solving abilities can lead to better time management and prioritization, reducing stress and anxiety associated with feeling overwhelmed or overburdened. It's easy to freak out when you're not thinking clearly due to overwhelming stress and anxiety in your life. Work and home life pressures can take over your time and understanding of your real priorities. Letting go of procrastination and embracing a proactive mindset can support more efficient and productive habits.

Healthier interpersonal relationships: Better decision-making and problem-solving skills can contribute to healthier interpersonal relationships, as individuals are more capable of effectively communicating their needs, resolving conflicts, and finding solutions to relational challenges. Having too much stress in your life will bleed negativity to those around you. You can quickly lash out at them, causing emotional harm, only to regret your burst of hurt later. Keeping calm and centered through the reduction of stress and anxiety will help prevent your sudden fits of anger. Letting go of past disappointments and focusing on building positive relationships can further enhance interpersonal connections and emotional well-being.

Greater goal achievement and personal growth: Improved decision-making and problem-solving abilities can support greater goal achievement and personal growth, as individuals are more likely to make choices that align with their values and priorities. Ever made a hasting decision when you're stressed out? Or setting some crazy goal just because? Your personal growth and goal setting can only be done effectively when your mind and body are centered correctly. High stress and anxiety levels will prevent you from choosing the right plan in life. Letting go of past failures and focusing on progress can foster a growth mindset and continued personal development.

Reduced rumination and overthinking: Better decision-making and problem-solving skills can help reduce rumination and overthinking, which often contribute to stress and anxiety. It can create a snowball effect of solving problems the wrong way. Being stressed out will keep you from thinking clearly and allowing inappropriate thoughts to run wildly through your mind. You can overthink the situation and create doubt about your ability to solve problems. Letting go of the need to overanalyze situations and embracing mindfulness practices can promote a more balanced and peaceful mental state.

Increased sense of satisfaction and well-being: As individuals develop more effective decision-making and problem-solving skills, they can experience increased satisfaction with their choices and greater overall well-being. You find peace in your life and the choices you make. Getting stuck in an over-stressed environment will prohibit your happiness, making you feel quite unsatisfied. Letting go of unneeded anxiety will put you in the right place to move forward and truly live the life you desire.

Better resource management: Improved decision-making and problem-solving abilities can lead to better resource management, both in personal and professional contexts. There's only so much time in the day to get things done, and being too stressed out won't help. You're anxious about all the tasks at hand, both at home and at work. You can easily feel overwhelmed by all of them, yet there's no one to turn to for help. That said, time is precious, and by letting go of the stress and anxiety, one can focus more clearly on the tasks and get them done more quickly. There will always be things needing to get done in life, but there may not always be you and your loved ones there. Prioritizing tasks and decisions are critical to living a full life. Letting go of the fear of scarcity and embracing abundance can further support effective resource allocation and stress reduction.

Enhanced creativity and innovation: Effective decision-making and problem-solving skills can foster creativity and innovation, as individuals are better able to think critically and explore new ideas and solutions. Have you ever been trying to solve a problem under immense pressure? How creative can you be with too much stress and anxiety in your life? Let it go. By doing so, you may be amazed at the innovation that seems to come out of nowhere and help resolve the issue. Letting go of limiting beliefs and embracing one's potential can support continued growth and self-discovery.

By practicing the art of letting go and focusing on improving decision-making and problem-solving skills, individuals can experience numerous benefits for reducing stress and anxiety, promoting greater well-being, resilience, and personal growth. Only then can you enjoy the happiness and excitement you long for in life. Dare to remove your stress and anxiety and think better – think differently.

Increased Relaxation

Increased relaxation is another benefit of letting go. Holding onto something can create a constant feeling of stress, leading to physical symptoms such as muscle tension and headaches, among other things. However, when we let go, we release that tension and can experience a greater sense of relaxation in our body and mind. This can positively impact our overall health and well-being and allow us to enjoy the present moment better.

Here are some key advantages of greater relaxation in terms of alleviating stress and anxiety, along with the associated benefits of letting go:

Lower stress levels: Relaxation techniques can help to lower the body's stress response, reducing the production of stress hormones like cortisol and adrenaline. Trying to deal with daily problems when your stress levels are high can be extremely difficult. It's not only bad for the mind but bad for the body. Spending a few minutes each day in a calm environment to relax can help alleviate the impacts on your body. This, in turn, can help relax your mind and allow you to function more properly. Letting go of excessive worry and negative thought patterns can further decrease stress levels and create a more balanced emotional state.

Improved emotional well-being: Increased relaxation can contribute to better emotional well-being, as individuals experience more positive emotions and a greater sense of calm and contentment. Keep calm and move on to the next thought. By removing the annoying negative thoughts in your head, you can focus on keeping your emotions in check. Let the thoughts travel – don't let them grow roots. Eventually, your emotional state will level off so you can enjoy the day. Letting go of emotional baggage and embracing acceptance can foster a more positive outlook and a stronger sense of inner peace.

Enhanced mental focus: Relaxation techniques can help to clear the mind and improve mental focus, making it easier to manage stressors and challenges more effectively. Listening to your mind seems crazy, but it's important to understand what the mind is trying to do. If the stress of life is reduced, you should eventually have better mental clarity. Relaxation will help break the brain fog so you can get on with your day. Letting go of distractions and unproductive thoughts can further sharpen mental clarity and promote better decision-making.

Better sleep quality: Increased relaxation can lead to improved sleep quality and duration, which is essential for overall mental and physical health, and can help to reduce stress and anxiety levels. Taking a few minutes before bedtime to sit in a quiet place and work through the stress of the day is important. Trying to do this in bed while you're trying to sleep is not ideal, but nonetheless, you must deal with the anxious thoughts at some point. Otherwise, you will have poor sleep quality. Letting go of racing thoughts and worries before bedtime can support a night of more restful and rejuvenating sleep.

Reduced physical tension: Relaxation techniques can help alleviate muscle tension and physical discomfort, often associated with stress and anxiety. Even though you may be dealing with stressful thoughts, they ultimately can affect your physical well-being. Spending time quietly relaxing can help remove mental stress and reduce physical stress festering in your muscles. Typically, the hard part is getting your mind to let go. But letting go of physical stress and consciously releasing tension can contribute to a greater sense of bodily comfort and relaxation.

Improved coping skills: Practicing relaxation can improve an individual's ability to cope with stress and anxiety by promoting a more balanced emotional state and increasing resilience. You generally have better ways of coping with stress when you're in a relaxed state. If you're anxious, you tend to do stupid things that won't inevitably help your situation. Letting go of unhelpful coping mechanisms and adopting healthier strategies can further enhance an individual's ability to manage stress.

Greater self-awareness: Relaxation techniques often involve mindfulness and self-awareness, helping individuals to recognize better and manage their stress and anxiety triggers. It's hard to be aware of yourself when dealing with high stress levels. Taking some time throughout the day to relax through meditation can help get you back to listening to your mind and body and be more aware of the bad things occurring. It can also help you recognize the good things as well. Letting go of self-judgment and embracing self-compassion can support a deeper understanding of one's emotions and reactions.

Enhanced immune function: Chronic stress and anxiety can suppress the immune system. Increased relaxation can help to counteract this effect, promoting better immune function and overall health. Being in a relaxed mood is like sleeping – your mind and body have time to reset and repair. This includes your immune system. Even if it's only a few minutes each day, preferably in the morning and before bedtime, your overall ability to fight disease is improved. Letting go of chronic stressors and finding healthier ways to cope can support a stronger immune system.

Lower blood pressure and heart rate: Relaxation techniques can help to lower blood pressure and heart rate, reducing the risk of stress-related health issues such as hypertension and cardiovascular disease. This should be obvious to everyone – the hard part is getting relaxed enough to show the results. Forcing yourself to relax is like forcing yourself not to think about something. Sure, you may get some short-term gains by pushing the thought away, but in time it comes back. When you let the thought come and go, it eventually will drift away. True relaxation cannot be forced – it must be cultivated in the right environment. Doing so can successfully lower things like blood pressure and heart rate.

Increased sense of control: By practicing relaxation techniques, individuals can gain greater control over their stress and anxiety levels, empowering them to manage their emotional well-being more effectively. You can be more centered and balanced by being in the right frame of mind through relaxation. You feel in control more. This does not mean you are in control of everything around you – the only thing you can control, for the most part, is your attitude. Being in a relaxed state of mind allows you to feel right with the world – control or not. Letting go of the need for constant control and embracing the present moment can foster a more balanced and peaceful state of mind.

By incorporating relaxation techniques and the practice of letting go into their daily routine, individuals can experience numerous benefits for reducing stress and anxiety and promoting better mental, emotional, and physical health. Mindful meditation and other tools are critical to relaxation and will be discussed in later chapters. Next, we'll spend some relaxing time discussing how letting go can help improve relationships in life.

CHAPTER 4
- IMPROVED
RELATIONSHIPS

Letting go of negative emotions can improve our relationships with others in several ways. When we're not holding onto negative energies like anger or hurt, we're able to connect with others from a place of caring, compassion, and understanding. Trying to have a conversation with others when you're in a bad place is not productive. Letting go of grudges and resentments can also help us communicate more effectively, as negative thoughts and feelings do not cloud us. Additionally, letting go can help us see things from different perspectives and be more open-minded, which can help us navigate conflicts and build stronger relationships. Letting go of negative emotions can create more space for love, kindness, and empathy in our relationships, which being social creatures at heart, is critical.

Let's investigate just a few specific ways that letting go can improve our relationships with others.

Increased Empathy

When we hold onto our own negative emotions, it can be difficult to understand and empathize with the experiences of others truly. But when we let go of our own biases and judgments, we create space for empathy and understanding to grow. This can improve our relationships by allowing us to connect with others on a deeper level and build a greater sense of trust and mutual respect. By letting go of our own negativity, we become more open to the experiences and perspectives of others, which can enrich our lives and the relationships we have with those around us.

Here are some key advantages of increased empathy in terms of enhancing relationships, along with the associated benefits of letting go:

Deeper emotional connections: Increased empathy can lead to deeper emotional connections, as individuals are better able to understand and relate to others' feelings and experiences. Putting yourself in someone else's shoes can go a long way. It can help you feel what others are feeling to some extent. It may remove some of your biases about what's important in the current situation and help you think about where they come from.

Letting go of judgment and embracing compassion can further strengthen emotional bonds and interpersonal relationships.

Improved communication: Greater empathy can contribute to improved communication, as empathetic individuals are more likely to listen actively, express understanding, and respond appropriately to others' needs. Listening is one of the most important activities you can do, yet most people are worried about not being heard. Everyone is trying to express themselves and feel important. Where does that put the others around you? Are you more important than them? In some respects, yes, as there's no you without you.

That said, we all have equal rights to be heard, so shut up and listen as best you can. Be aware of you taking over conversations too much. Letting go of the need to be right and embracing open-mindedness can further enhance communication and understanding within relationships.

Enhanced conflict resolution: Increased empathy can help in resolving conflicts more effectively, as empathetic individuals are more likely to approach disagreements with understanding and a willingness to find common ground. When you walk into a room with a preset idea of how to resolve an issue, you may be wrong.

Listening is critical to the process. Let others express themselves and work together to find the solution. Letting go of defensiveness and embracing collaboration can further promote constructive conflict resolution and relationship growth.

Greater emotional support: Empathetic individuals can provide greater emotional support to their loved ones, as they are more in tune with others' emotions and needs. Empathy provides a way to try your best to know what the other person is truly thinking and feeling. Listen to their wants and needs, then work with them – not against them to find the answers.

Letting go of the need to fix others' problems and embracing a supportive and validating approach can strengthen emotional connections and well-being within relationships.

Increased trust and intimacy: Greater empathy within relationships can lead to increased trust and intimacy as individuals feel more understood, valued, and supported by their partners. If you shut others out in a conversation, they lose trust in you. They won't confide in their true feelings and reject any thoughts they may have. Be open to those around you through empathy; you will be surprised at the level of trust and intimacy you receive. It does, however, go both ways. If you are not feeling a sense of trust back, do your best to provide compassion. Letting go of fear and vulnerability and embracing emotional openness can further deepen trust and intimacy.

Better understanding of diverse perspectives: Increased empathy allows individuals to understand diverse perspectives better, fostering greater tolerance and acceptance within relationships. You will not always come to a mutual agreement, but that doesn't mean either of you are right or wrong. Use empathy to understand better where they are coming from.

Agree to disagree if you must. But don't blow them off because they have a different perspective on life. Letting go of rigid thinking patterns and embracing curiosity can further promote open-mindedness and understanding.

Enhanced teamwork and collaboration: Empathy can contribute to enhanced teamwork and collaboration, as individuals are more likely to appreciate others' strengths, contributions, and viewpoints. No man is an island. We are social creatures for a reason. Being open-minded about trying to get things done is critical to finding solutions and enjoying life.

Listening and asking questions in a positive manner will provide a resolution to problems you might be amazed at. Letting go of competition and embracing cooperation can further support collaborative and harmonious relationships.

Reduced stress and increased emotional well-being: Greater empathy can lead to reduced stress and increased emotional well-being within relationships, as individuals feel more understood and supported by their loved ones. Empathy can reward your productivity and enjoyment throughout the day, even at work.

By practicing empathy, the heated debates dissolve and open the door to lower levels of stress. Emotionally you feel more at ease. Checking your ego at the door for work is always a good idea. At home too. Letting go of unrealistic expectations and embracing acceptance can further promote emotional balance and overall well-being.

Increased personal growth and self-awareness: As individuals develop greater empathy, they can also experience increased personal growth and self-awareness as they become more attuned to their own emotions and reactions. Empathy is not a one-way street. It works both ways.

Practicing empathy with others can eventually improve your growth in life and make you more aware of who you are. Letting go of self-criticism and embracing self-compassion can support continued growth and self-discovery.

Greater relationship satisfaction: Enhanced empathy can contribute to greater relationship satisfaction, as individuals feel more connected, supported, and valued by their partners. Listening, in many cases, is more important than talking. It can help build trust and love in a relationship.

This can drive conversations in a more meaningful way and provide a greater sense of satisfaction with your partner. Don't focus too much on negative past experiences. Letting go of past disappointments and building positive relationships can further enhance overall satisfaction and happiness.

Reduced Conflict

Holding onto negative emotions, such as anger or resentment, can create tension and conflict in our relationships with others. Letting go of these emotions can help us avoid unnecessary arguments and disagreements, leading to more peaceful and rewarding relationships. Additionally, letting go of our own biases can increase our ability to empathize with others and see things from their viewpoint. This can further reduce conflict by promoting understanding and communication. Ultimately, learning to let go can lead to more positive and fulfilling relationships with others.

Here are some key advantages of reduced conflict in terms of enhancing relationships, along with the associated benefits of letting go:

Enhanced emotional well-being: Enhanced emotional well-being is one of the most significant benefits of learning to let go in relationships. Individuals can experience a greater sense of inner peace and contentment by reducing conflict and tension. Holding onto negative emotions such as resentment can be emotionally draining and create an overall negative atmosphere in our relationships. By practicing forgiveness and letting go of grudges, we can release these negative emotions and promote a more positive environment.

Let's say you have a friend who canceled plans with you at the last minute, leaving you feeling frustrated and disappointed. If you hold onto that resentment and continue to dwell on it, it can create tension and conflict between you and your friend. However, if you choose to let go of that negative emotion and practice forgiveness, you can move past the incident and maintain a positive relationship with your friend. This can promote emotional well-being and prevent unnecessary conflict in the future.

By practicing letting go in relationships, we can promote

emotional balance, improve communication, and foster more positive and fulfilling relationships.

Improved communication: Improved communication is one of the key benefits of learning to let go in relationships. Holding onto negative emotions, such as anger, frustration, or resentment, can create a barrier in communication with others. These negative emotions can cause us to become defensive or closed off to other perspectives, making it difficult to engage in open and honest conversations. However, we can approach conversations with a more open and understanding mindset when we learn to let go of these negative emotions.

If someone in a romantic relationship is feeling hurt or neglected by their partner, they may initially respond with defensiveness or anger. But if they can let go of these emotions and approach the conversation with a more open and empathetic mindset, they may be able to have a more productive conversation that leads to greater understanding and resolution.

In addition to letting go of negative emotions, actively practicing skills such as active listening can also enhance communication within relationships. Active listening involves fully focusing on the speaker, refraining from interrupting or judging, and seeking to understand their perspective. By embracing active listening and letting go of defensiveness, individuals can improve their ability to communicate effectively and build stronger, more fulfilling relationships.

Greater trust and security: When individuals let go of their need to be right, they become more open to understanding other people's perspectives. This willingness to understand can increase empathy and reduce the likelihood of arguments or misunderstandings, ultimately promoting greater trust and emotional security within relationships.

Imagine a couple who always argue about how to spend their weekends. One partner insists on spending every weekend relaxing at home, while the other wants to go out and be more social. Instead of getting defensive and trying to prove their point, they can let go of the need to be right and listen to each other's perspectives. Through active listening and empathizing with their partner's desires, they may come up with a compromise that satisfies both, ultimately strengthening their trust and emotional security.

By letting go of the need to be right and embracing empathy, individuals can create a more secure and trusting environment within their relationships. This can lead to deeper connections and a more fulfilling life.

Stronger emotional connections: Strong emotional connections are crucial for maintaining healthy and fulfilling relationships. When conflict is minimized, individuals are more likely to focus on the positive aspects of their relationships and appreciate each other's strengths. This can lead to a deeper understanding and empathy toward one another.

For instance, let's say a married couple has had a history of arguments about finances. However, they decide to work on letting go of the past and instead choose to focus on their shared values and goals. Doing so can strengthen their emotional connection and work together towards a brighter future.

Practicing gratitude can also deepen emotional bonds by encouraging individuals to focus on the positive aspects of their relationships.

Increased relationship satisfaction: Reducing conflict and increasing positive behaviors such as acceptance, empathy, and gratitude can lead to greater relationship satisfaction. When partners feel heard and understood, they are more likely to feel valued and respected, leading to a deeper connection and sense of intimacy.

Let's say a couple has been arguing frequently over household chores. By letting go of their defensiveness and actively listening to each other's concerns, they can come up with a more equitable division of labor. This leads to a reduction in conflict, increased trust, and improved communication, ultimately resulting in greater relationship satisfaction.

Greater personal growth and self-awareness: Reduced conflict can also provide an opportunity for personal growth and self-awareness by allowing individuals to focus on their own needs and desires. By letting go of negative emotions and conflicts within a relationship, individuals may begin to recognize patterns in their own behavior and communication style. A person may notice that they tend to be defensive or avoidant when conflicts arise and may begin to work on developing more assertive and effective communication skills.

Additionally, letting go of negative emotions and conflicts can help individuals to gain a deeper understanding of their own values and beliefs, as well as those of their partner. This increased self-awareness can support continued personal growth and development.

Enhanced teamwork and collaboration: When individuals in a relationship experience reduced conflict, they are more likely to work together towards common goals, which can lead to enhanced teamwork and collaboration.

Imagine a work team where two members have had an ongoing conflict that has hindered the team's progress. When they let go of their differences and adopt a more cooperative mindset, they are more likely to collaborate effectively and contribute to the team's overall success. Embracing a collaborative approach and letting go of competition can also promote a more positive team culture, where everyone feels valued and respected, and team members are motivated to support each other's success.

Better problem-solving and conflict resolution: When individuals experience lower levels of conflict within their relationships, they are more likely to engage in better problem-solving and conflict resolution strategies. This is because they are better able to approach challenges with an open and collaborative mindset. When individuals let go of the need to be right or win arguments, they can embrace compromise and constructive resolution of disagreements.

In a workplace setting, two colleagues may have different ideas on how to approach a project. If they approach the situation with defensiveness and a need to be right, it can quickly escalate into conflict. However, if they let go of the need to be right and embrace active listening, they can work together to find a solution that incorporates the strengths of both ideas. By adopting a collaborative mindset, they can reach a compromise that satisfies both parties and leads to a successful outcome.

Effective problem-solving and conflict resolution can lead to greater emotional safety and satisfaction in personal relationships. When individuals can work through disagreements in a constructive manner, it can promote a sense of trust and respect within the relationship. This can lead to a deeper emotional connection and a stronger sense of partnership.

Increased resilience and coping skills: When individuals experience less conflict within their relationships, they may develop stronger resilience and coping skills. For instance, if a couple faces a stressful situation such as a job loss or a health issue, they may be better equipped to navigate the challenge by working together and supporting each other. They may also better understand each other's needs and coping mechanisms, which can help them offer more effective support. This can promote better stress management and improved emotional well-being over time.

For example, if one partner loses their job, the other partner may actively listen and offer emotional support instead of blaming them or becoming defensive. By working together and exploring different options, they may come up with a plan to manage their finances and find new job opportunities. This can reduce stress and anxiety and deepen their emotional connection and trust. In contrast, if they respond with criticism and blame, the stress and tension may increase and strain their relationship.

More enjoyable and fulfilling relationships: When individuals experience less conflict within their relationships, they tend to enjoy their connections more fully. They can appreciate the positive aspects of their relationships and focus on building meaningful and satisfying bonds. By letting go of past disappointments and focusing on the present moment, individuals can enhance their relationship satisfaction and happiness.

Let's say that a couple has been struggling with constant arguments and disagreements over various issues. The arguments have led to feelings of frustration and disappointment on both sides. However, after working on letting go of negative emotions and adopting more positive coping strategies, the couple begins to experience less conflict and more positive interactions. They are better able to communicate their needs and appreciate each other's strengths, leading to a deeper sense of connection and enjoyment in their relationship. As a result, they can create a more fulfilling and satisfying bond with each other.

Better Communication

When we're holding onto negative emotions, it can be difficult to communicate effectively with others. We may be defensive or closed off, which can make it hard for us to listen to what they're saying. But when we let go of those negative emotions, we can approach conversations more openly. We're more likely to be good listeners and better able to communicate our own thoughts and feelings. This can lead to more productive, positive conversations, which can strengthen our relationships with others.

Here are some key advantages of better communication in terms of enhancing relationships, along with the associated benefits of letting go:

Greater emotional connection: Effective communication is essential for building strong emotional connections within relationships. When individuals can express their thoughts, feelings, and needs in an open and honest way, they create a foundation of trust and understanding that can deepen their connection. By letting go of defensiveness and embracing vulnerability, individuals can further enhance their emotional connection and build stronger relationships.

Let's say a couple is having trouble communicating about a difficult issue in their relationship. One partner may feel defensive or unwilling to listen to the other's perspective, which can lead to frustration and a lack of resolution. By letting go of defensiveness and actively listening to their partner's point of view, they can begin to understand each other's needs and work towards a solution that benefits both. This type of communication fosters a deeper emotional connection and strengthens their relationship.

Improved conflict resolution: Improved conflict resolution is a significant benefit of effective communication in relationships. When individuals communicate well, they can understand and acknowledge each other's concerns, which can help to de-escalate the conflict. They can also work together to find mutually agreeable solutions to their problems rather than blaming each other for their issues.

For instance, imagine a situation where two friends have different opinions about where to go for dinner. Instead of arguing or shutting down, they can use effective communication to understand each other's preferences and come up with a mutually agreeable solution. They can let go of their individual viewpoints and embrace collaboration, ultimately finding a restaurant that they both enjoy. By resolving their conflict constructively, they have a satisfying dining experience and strengthen their friendship through effective communication.

Increased trust and intimacy: Effective communication can help to build trust and intimacy in relationships. When individuals feel safe expressing their thoughts and feelings, it creates a deeper emotional connection.

A couple who has difficulty communicating their needs and desires may struggle with intimacy. However, if they work on improving their communication skills and learn to listen to each other without judgment, they may be able to develop a deeper level of emotional intimacy.

Letting go of fear and vulnerability is important to building trust and intimacy. When individuals are willing to share their thoughts and feelings, it creates a safe space for their partner to do the same. If one partner is afraid to share their vulnerabilities with the other, it can create a barrier to intimacy. However, if they work on letting go of that fear and being open with each other, it can lead to greater emotional closeness and intimacy.

Overall, effective communication is essential for building trust and intimacy in relationships. By letting go of fear and vulnerability and embracing emotional openness and collaboration, individuals can create deeper connections and stronger relationships with their partners.

Enhanced empathy and understanding: Enhanced empathy and understanding are key components of healthy and fulfilling relationships. Effective communication is the foundation upon which empathy and understanding can be built. When individuals can communicate effectively, they can learn to understand each other's perspectives and empathize with each other's experiences.

A couple may have a disagreement about how to spend their free time. Instead of becoming defensive or dismissive, they can practice active listening and ask questions to understand each other's needs and desires better. Through this process, they may discover that one partner values quality time together while the other enjoys alone time. By understanding each other's perspectives, they can work together to find a solution that meets both of their needs.

Letting go of preconceptions and embracing curiosity is also important for enhancing empathy and understanding. When individuals let go of assumptions and preconceived notions, they are better able to approach their partners with an open mind and a willingness to learn.

Healthier interpersonal relationships: Effective communication is essential for building healthy interpersonal relationships. When individuals communicate effectively, they are better able to express their needs and concerns, resolve conflicts, and find solutions to relational challenges. Effective communication also promotes understanding and empathy, which can help to strengthen emotional connections within relationships.

A couple may have been struggling to communicate their needs and concerns effectively. They may have been avoiding difficult conversations, leading to unresolved conflicts and tension in the relationship. By learning how to communicate more effectively, they can express their needs and concerns clearly and respectfully, leading to greater understanding and connection.

Letting go of judgment and embracing compassion is also important in building healthier relationships. When individuals let go of their preconceptions and biases and approach others with an open mind and heart, they are better able to connect with them on a deeper level. This can lead to more meaningful and fulfilling relationships.

Increased relationship satisfaction: Effective communication is key to maintaining a healthy and satisfying relationship. When couples communicate well, they are more likely to feel heard, understood, and appreciated by their partner. This can lead to greater relationship satisfaction and happiness.

Consider a couple who is struggling to spend quality time together due to their busy schedules. By using effective communication, they can express their desire to spend time together and work towards finding a solution that works for both. Maybe they decide to have a weekly date night or plan a weekend getaway to reconnect and strengthen their bond. By prioritizing their relationship and communicating effectively, they can increase their overall satisfaction and happiness in the relationship.

Additionally, effective communication can help couples navigate other relational challenges, such as disagreements about finances, parenting styles, or career decisions. By being open, honest, and respectful in their communication, couples can work together to find solutions that promote mutual growth and happiness.

Enhanced self-awareness: Effective communication can promote enhanced self-awareness as individuals learn to recognize their communication patterns, including their strengths and weaknesses. By paying close attention to how they communicate and receive information, individuals can become more self-aware and better able to understand their own feelings, thoughts, and needs.

Let's say someone tends to interrupt others during conversations. By recognizing this pattern and how it impacts their interactions with others, they can take steps to improve their communication skills and become more self-aware of their behavior. They may start practicing active listening, listening attentively to what the other person is saying and responding thoughtfully. This can help them become more present in the moment and be more conscious of their own communication style.

Similarly, practicing effective communication can also help individuals become more aware of their emotions and how they impact their communication.

Someone may notice that they tend to shut down during conflict or become defensive when criticized. By recognizing these patterns and working to change them, they can become more self-aware of their emotional triggers and learn to communicate more effectively in difficult situations.

Overall, effective communication can promote self-awareness, which can support personal growth and development. By letting go of self-criticism and embracing self-compassion, individuals can continue to learn and improve their communication skills, leading to healthier and more fulfilling relationships.

Improved decision-making: Effective communication within relationships can lead to improved decision-making for the individuals involved. When partners engage in open, respectful communication, they are better equipped to discuss and explore all the available options, which can help them make informed decisions. Moreover, this type of communication promotes trust, mutual respect, and a better understanding of each other's values, needs, and priorities.

For instance, let's consider a couple deciding whether to relocate for a new job opportunity. They can share their thoughts, concerns, and priorities about the move through effective communication. They can openly discuss the potential benefits and drawbacks and brainstorm solutions to any challenges. They can also ensure that their decision aligns with their shared values and goals for the future. By working collaboratively through the decision-making process, the couple can feel more confident in their choice and experience greater satisfaction with the outcome.

In contrast, ineffective communication may lead to misunderstandings, unspoken concerns, and a lack of trust. This can result in hasty or poorly informed decisions, which may not align with the needs or desires of both partners, leading to dissatisfaction and potential conflict in the future.

Thus, by letting go of the need to be right and embracing a collaborative approach to decision-making, individuals can experience the benefits of effective communication within their relationships.

Increased personal growth and self-esteem: Effective communication skills can contribute to increased personal growth and self-esteem. When individuals can express themselves clearly and confidently, they are more likely to feel empowered and in control of their lives. Through effective communication, individuals can better understand their own values, beliefs, and needs and work towards aligning their actions with their authentic selves.

Imagine an individual who struggles with low self-esteem and finds it difficult to express themselves in social situations. Through learning and practicing effective communication skills, they may become more comfortable with expressing their opinions and needs, leading to greater self-confidence and self-esteem. As a result, they may feel more comfortable asserting their boundaries and pursuing their goals, leading to a more fulfilling and satisfying life.

Letting go of self-doubt and embracing self-confidence can further support personal growth and self-esteem. By recognizing and challenging negative self-talk and beliefs, individuals can shift towards a more positive and empowering mindset, promoting greater self-awareness and personal development.

More enjoyable and fulfilling relationships: Effective communication is key to building enjoyable and fulfilling relationships. By communicating effectively, individuals can connect with each other, understand each other's needs and perspectives, and provide support. This can lead to a deeper sense of intimacy and fulfillment within the relationship.

Imagine a couple who have been together for several years but have been experiencing increasing levels of tension and disagreement. They decide to seek counseling to work on their communication skills. Through the counseling process, they learn to communicate more effectively, listen actively, and express their feelings in a constructive way. As a result, they begin to understand each other better, support each other more effectively, and feel more connected and fulfilled in their relationship.

By letting go of unproductive communication patterns, such as defensiveness, blame, and criticism, and embracing more positive and constructive approaches, such as active listening, empathy, and collaboration, individuals can build stronger and more enjoyable relationships with their loved ones.

Greater Trust

When we hold onto grudges or negative emotions towards someone, it can make it difficult to trust them. We may be suspicious of their motives or doubt their intentions. However, when we let go of these negative emotions, we create space for trust to grow. We're more open to seeing the good in others and believing in their intentions. In turn, they're more likely to trust us as well. This can lead to stronger and more meaningful relationships built on a foundation of trust and mutual respect.

Here are some key advantages of greater trust in terms of enhancing relationships, along with the associated benefits of letting go:

Enhanced emotional connection: When we trust someone, we feel safe enough to open to them and share our innermost thoughts and feelings. This can lead to a deeper level of emotional connection and intimacy within the relationship.

Let's say that a couple has been together for a few years, but they have always struggled with fully trusting each other. One partner may have insecurities about the other's fidelity, while the other may feel guarded about sharing personal information. However, over time, they begin to work on building trust by being honest and open with each other. As a result, they begin to feel more connected on an emotional level and can share their thoughts and feelings more freely, leading to a stronger bond.

Letting go of fear and embracing vulnerability is key to building trust and enhancing emotional connection. It requires us to be open and honest with ourselves and our partners and be willing to take risks to build deeper connections. Doing so allows us to experience greater emotional intimacy and fulfillment in our relationships.

Improved communication: Greater trust can indeed

contribute to improved communication within relationships. When individuals trust each other, they are more likely to be open and honest with each other. They are also more likely to listen carefully and with an open mind to what their partner has to say rather than jumping to conclusions or becoming defensive.

For instance, a couple may have struggled with communication around a sensitive topic such as parenting styles. As they work on building trust, they begin to communicate more openly and honestly about their perspectives on parenting. They let go of any judgment or being defensive and actively listen to each other's ideas. Over time, this improved communication helps them better understand each other's priorities and strengthens their relationship.

In this way, letting go of past hurts and embracing trust can foster improved communication and greater relationship satisfaction.

Stronger emotional support: Stronger emotional support is one of the many benefits of trust in a relationship. When individuals trust their partners, they feel more comfortable sharing their thoughts and feelings and seek support during challenging times. This emotional support can come in the form of listening, validation, and encouragement, which can help individuals cope with stress and build resilience.

Imagine a couple who have been together for a few years. One partner experiences a setback at work and is feeling stressed and overwhelmed. They turn to their partner for emotional support, and instead of being dismissive or critical, the partner listens actively, offers empathy, and helps brainstorm solutions. This emotional support strengthens the relationship, promotes a sense of security, and helps the individual manage stress more effectively.

Letting go of self-reliance and embracing interdependence is essential for building trust and fostering emotional support. This means recognizing that it's okay to rely on others for support and that seeking help is a sign of strength, not weakness. In turn, providing emotional support to others can also strengthen trust and deepen emotional connections within relationships.

Enhanced conflict resolution: When trust is established within a relationship, conflict resolution can become more effective and productive. Trust can create a safe and secure environment where individuals feel comfortable expressing their feelings and concerns without fear of judgment or negative consequences.

Trust can help partners navigate disagreements and find mutually beneficial solutions in a romantic relationship. When trust is present, partners may be more willing to listen actively, respect each other's perspectives, and work together to find common ground. They may also be more likely to forgive each other and move past conflicts, knowing that they can rely on each other for support and understanding.

Letting go of defensiveness and embracing vulnerability can further enhance conflict resolution within a relationship. When individuals let go of the need to be right and instead focus on understanding and collaboration, they can approach conflict with a more constructive and open mindset. This can lead to a more positive and rewarding relationship dynamic, where conflicts are seen as opportunities for growth and understanding rather than threats to the relationship.

Increased intimacy and sexual satisfaction: When individuals feel a sense of trust within their relationships, they are more likely to feel comfortable exploring their sexual desires and being open with their partners about their needs. This can lead to increased intimacy and sexual satisfaction within the relationship.

A couple who has built a strong foundation of trust and openness may feel more comfortable discussing their sexual preferences, leading to a more fulfilling and satisfying sexual experience for both partners. Additionally, greater trust and emotional connection can lead to more frequent and meaningful physical touch, which can further enhance intimacy and relationship satisfaction.

Greater personal growth and self-awareness: When individuals trust their partners, they may feel more comfortable being vulnerable and sharing personal experiences or thoughts. This can create a safe and supportive environment where individuals can learn and grow from each other. Additionally, as individuals work through challenges and disagreements together, they may gain a deeper understanding of their own values, needs, and communication patterns. By reflecting on these experiences, they can develop greater self-awareness and identify areas for personal growth.

Consider a couple who has been together for several years but has struggled with trust issues in the past. As they work to build trust and strengthen their relationship, they may engage in open and honest communication, share their fears and insecurities, and work together to find solutions. Through this process, they may learn more about their own patterns of communication, such as when they tend to become defensive or how they can better express their needs. As they develop greater self-awareness, they can work towards creating a healthier and more fulfilling relationship.

Enhanced teamwork and collaboration: In relationships, trust is a critical component of successful teamwork and collaboration. When individuals trust each other, they are more willing to rely on each other's strengths and work together towards common goals. This can result in more effective problem-solving, greater efficiency, and a sense of shared accomplishment.

In a business partnership, trusting each other's abilities and intentions can lead to more productive brainstorming sessions, a better delegation of tasks, and a more streamlined approach to achieving business objectives. When each partner feels secure in their role and their relationship with their partner, they are more likely to work together with a sense of cooperation and mutual respect.

In personal relationships, greater trust can also lead to enhanced teamwork and collaboration in tasks such as planning events, organizing a household, or raising children. When partners trust each other to fulfill their responsibilities and support each other through challenges, they can work together to create a harmonious and satisfying home life.

Letting go of competition and embracing cooperation can further support teamwork and collaboration by promoting a shared focus on achieving common goals. Instead of viewing each other as adversaries, individuals can work together as partners to accomplish more than they would on their own. This can lead to a greater sense of unity and fulfillment within the relationship.

Increased relationship satisfaction: Greater trust can create a stronger foundation for a relationship, leading to increased relationship satisfaction. When there is trust, individuals can rely on each other and feel more secure in the relationship. This can lead to greater intimacy and a deeper emotional connection, as both individuals feel comfortable being vulnerable with each other.

Let's say a couple has had conflicts around boundaries in their relationship, causing mistrust and tension. By setting clear boundaries and being consistent in respecting them, they can rebuild trust and create a stronger foundation for their relationship. As they rely on each other more and feel more secure in the relationship, they experience greater intimacy and emotional connection. They may feel more comfortable sharing their innermost thoughts and feelings with each other, leading to increased relationship satisfaction and happiness.

Furthermore, when individuals trust their partners, they may also feel more comfortable expressing their needs and desires, leading to a more fulfilling relationship. When both individuals are committed to building trust and supporting each other, they can create a positive and satisfying relationship dynamic.

Enhanced self-esteem and confidence: When individuals experience greater trust within their relationships, they feel more secure and valued, which can contribute to enhanced self-esteem and confidence. This sense of validation and support from their partners can help individuals feel more comfortable expressing themselves and pursuing their goals.

If someone has been hesitant to pursue a new career path, feeling supported and validated by their partner can give them the confidence to take the necessary steps to pursue their dreams. Additionally, feeling valued and respected within their relationships can help individuals develop a stronger sense of self-worth, leading to increased confidence in their abilities and decisions. By letting go of self-doubt and embracing self-love, individuals can continue to grow and develop a strong sense of self-worth and self-assurance.

More enjoyable and fulfilling relationships: Greater trust is vital to any healthy and fulfilling relationship. When trust is present, individuals are more likely to feel secure and supported in their relationship, leading to greater enjoyment and satisfaction. Additionally, a lack of trust can lead to conflict and tension, which can create an unhealthy dynamic within the relationship.

An example of how greater trust can lead to more enjoyable and fulfilling relationships is when a couple works to build trust in their relationship after a breach of trust, such as infidelity. In this scenario, the betrayed partner may initially struggle to trust their partner again, leading to tension and discomfort in the relationship. However, if the partner who breached trust takes responsibility for their actions, makes amends, and demonstrates consistent, trustworthy behavior, the betrayed partner may gradually begin to trust them again.

As trust is rebuilt, the couple can enjoy a deeper and more fulfilling connection as they feel secure and supported by each other. The process of rebuilding trust can also strengthen the relationship as the couple learns to communicate more openly and honestly and develop greater empathy and understanding for each other.

Letting go of negative beliefs or assumptions about the relationship and actively working towards building trust can further enhance relationship satisfaction and enjoyment. This can involve regularly expressing appreciation and gratitude for each other, being transparent and honest about one's actions and feelings, and consistently following through on commitments and promises. By building trust, individuals can experience a more fulfilling and rewarding relationship filled with positive interactions and shared experiences.

Improved Intimacy

When we let go of negative emotions like resentment, anger, or hurt, we become more open and vulnerable with others. This vulnerability can allow us to deepen our emotional connections and create more meaningful intimacy. When we hold onto negative emotions, we may put up walls and barriers that prevent us from truly opening up to others. Letting go creates space for trust and vulnerability, which can lead to deeper intimacy in our relationships. We become more authentic and honest with ourselves and our partners, allowing us to connect on a deeper level. Letting go can be scary, but it can also be incredibly rewarding in terms of intimacy and emotional connection.

Here are some key advantages of improved intimacy in terms of enhancing relationships, along with the associated benefits of letting go:

Greater emotional connection: Improved intimacy can enhance emotional connection within relationships in several ways. When partners are physically intimate, they are not just engaging in a physical act but also sharing their emotions, vulnerabilities, and desires with each other. This exchange of emotions and thoughts can create a sense of closeness and emotional connection between partners.

Moreover, improved intimacy often leads to more open communication and emotional expression between partners. When individuals feel more comfortable sharing their thoughts and feelings with their partners, it can create a deeper level of emotional connection and understanding. This emotional connection can further enhance the relationship's strength and resilience in the face of challenges and difficulties.

For instance, a couple who has been struggling to connect emotionally due to a lack of physical intimacy may decide to work on improving their intimacy by being more open about their desires and fears. They may let go of their fears of judgment and embrace vulnerability by expressing their feelings and needs more honestly with each other. As a result, they may experience a deeper level of emotional connection and closeness in their relationship.

By letting go of their fears and embracing vulnerability, they may also create a safe space where they can discuss and work through any issues that may arise in their relationship. This can lead to improved conflict resolution, increased trust, and greater emotional security within the relationship.

Enhanced trust: When individuals experience improved intimacy within their relationships, it can lead to enhanced trust between them and their partners. As they become more comfortable sharing their vulnerabilities and opening up emotionally, they can begin to build a stronger foundation of trust.

A couple may have difficulty discussing certain sensitive topics, such as their insecurities or past traumas. However, as they develop more intimacy and emotional connection, they may find it easier to have those conversations and trust that their partner will listen without judgment. Letting go of fear and embracing trust can further solidify the emotional bond and deepen their relationship.

Better communication: Improved intimacy can indeed lead to better communication within relationships. When individuals feel closer to their partners and more comfortable sharing their thoughts and feelings, they are more likely to communicate openly and honestly. This can help to build deeper understanding and trust and ultimately lead to a more fulfilling and satisfying relationship.

A couple that has struggled with communication may find that as they become more intimate and comfortable with each other, they are better able to express their needs and desires. They may feel more confident in sharing their vulnerabilities and fears, and in turn, their partner may respond with empathy and support. Over time, this can lead to a stronger emotional bond and a deeper sense of connection.

Letting go of shame and fear of judgment can also play an important role in enhancing communication within intimate relationships. When individuals feel comfortable expressing themselves without fear of criticism or rejection, they are more likely to communicate openly and honestly. This can help to build trust and emotional intimacy and create a more positive and fulfilling relationship.

Increased sexual satisfaction: Improved intimacy within a relationship can also lead to increased sexual satisfaction. When individuals feel more comfortable and connected with their partner, they are more likely to explore and express their sexual desires and preferences. This can lead to a deeper understanding of each other's needs and wants and can create a more fulfilling sexual experience for both partners.

A couple who has struggled with intimacy issues may start to work on building trust and emotional connection through open communication and vulnerability. As they become more comfortable expressing their desires and needs, they may discover new ways to enhance their sexual experience and bring more pleasure to each other. This can lead to a more satisfying and fulfilling sexual relationship and a deeper emotional connection outside of the bedroom.

Enhanced emotional support: When partners in a relationship feel emotionally connected, they are more likely to support and validate each other's feelings and needs. Improved intimacy can lead to enhanced emotional support within relationships.

Letting go of self-reliance and embracing interdependence can further promote emotional connection and well-being. This means that instead of relying solely on oneself for emotional support, one is willing to turn to their partner for help when needed. This can be challenging for some people, especially if they have a history of being independent or self-sufficient.

However, by letting go of the need always to be in control and embracing vulnerability, individuals can build deeper emotional connections and experience greater emotional support within their relationships.

Greater personal growth and self-awareness: Improved intimacy within relationships can lead to greater personal growth and self-awareness as individuals learn more about themselves and their partners through deepening their emotional and physical connections. As individuals feel more comfortable expressing their thoughts, feelings, and desires, they may gain a deeper understanding of their own needs and preferences, as well as those of their partners.

A couple may have struggled with intimacy in the past due to unresolved emotional issues or communication barriers. As they build trust and improve communication, they may feel more comfortable expressing their desires and exploring new ways of connecting intimately. This process can lead to a greater sense of self-awareness as everyone learns more about their own needs and desires, as well as those of their partner.

Letting go of self-judgment and embracing self-acceptance can support continued personal growth and self-discovery in the context of an intimate relationship. This can involve becoming more comfortable with vulnerability and emotional openness, as well as being willing to receive feedback and work through challenges together. As individuals learn more about themselves and their partners by deepening their emotional and physical connections, they may gain a deeper self-awareness and personal growth.

Enhanced teamwork and collaboration: Improved intimacy can lead to enhanced teamwork and collaboration within relationships because a deeper emotional connection can lead to a greater understanding and appreciation of each other's strengths and weaknesses. When partners feel more comfortable with each other, they can work together more effectively towards common goals.

A couple who shares a deep emotional connection may work better as a team when facing a challenge, such as planning a big event or managing finances. They can communicate their ideas and concerns openly, listen actively to each other, and find solutions that work for both. Letting go of competitiveness and embracing cooperation can further enhance their ability to work together and achieve their goals as a team.

Increased relationship satisfaction: When individuals experience improved intimacy in their relationship, they may feel more emotionally connected and fulfilled, leading to increased satisfaction. They may feel that they can trust their partner more and that they have a stronger bond.

A couple who has been experiencing communication difficulties may work on improving their intimacy by spending more quality time together, listening to each other, and expressing their needs and feelings. Doing so may make them feel more connected and happier in their relationship. The act of prioritizing intimacy and building a deeper connection can lead to increased relationship satisfaction and happiness.

Enhanced self-esteem and confidence: Improved intimacy within relationships can help increase an individual's self-esteem and confidence. When a person feels appreciated and loved by their partner, it can boost their sense of self-worth and value. This can lead to a greater sense of confidence in oneself and in the relationship.

If someone feels appreciated and loved by their partner, they may feel more confident in expressing their opinions and desires within the relationship. They may also feel more confident in pursuing personal goals and aspirations, knowing they have the support and encouragement of their partner.

Letting go of self-doubt and negative self-talk can further support this growth in self-esteem and confidence. By reframing one's thoughts and beliefs about oneself, individuals can start to see themselves in a more positive and affirming light. This can help break negative thinking patterns and promote greater self-acceptance and self-love.

More enjoyable and fulfilling relationships: Improved intimacy within a relationship can lead to more enjoyable and fulfilling experiences as the individuals involved feel more connected and supported by their partners.

A couple who has improved their intimacy through open communication and trust might find that they enjoy spending more quality time together. They might also find that they are able to express themselves more freely and creatively, leading to new shared experiences and a deeper sense of mutual fulfillment.

Additionally, improved intimacy can lead to greater emotional support during times of stress or hardship, as individuals feel more comfortable relying on their partners for understanding and encouragement. Overall, a relationship with improved intimacy can bring both partners a sense of joy, satisfaction, and meaning.

CHAPTER 5 - GREATER SENSE OF INNER PEACE

Letting go of the past, negative emotions, or limiting beliefs can help us find greater inner peace and contentment. When we're not constantly obsessing over the past or worrying about the future, we're able to be more present in the moment and appreciate the beauty of life.

By letting go of what no longer serves us, we can create more space for positive emotions like gratitude, joy, and love. This can help us find greater fulfillment and happiness in life. Additionally, when we let go of the need to control everything, we can find a sense of surrender and acceptance that can lead to greater peace.

Here are a few specific ways that letting go can improve your sense of inner peace:

Increased Mindfulness

Increased mindfulness is another benefit of letting go. When we hold onto things from the past, it can make it difficult to be fully present in the moment. We may be preoccupied with negative thoughts or worries about the future. Letting go can help us release these mental distractions and focus on the present. This can lead to a greater sense of peace and contentment and help us appreciate the simple joys of life. When we practice mindfulness, we're also more likely to be aware of our thoughts and emotions, which can help us make healthier choices and develop more positive habits.

Here are some key advantages of increased mindfulness in terms of enhancing inner peace, along with the associated benefits of letting go:

Reduced stress and anxiety: Mindfulness is the practice of being present and fully engaged in the current moment without judgment or distraction. When individuals incorporate mindfulness into their daily lives, they may experience a range of benefits, including reduced stress and anxiety. By focusing on the present moment and becoming more aware of their thoughts and emotions, individuals can learn to respond to them in a more balanced and centered way rather than becoming overwhelmed by them.

For example, if a person is feeling anxious about an upcoming presentation at work, they can practice mindfulness techniques such as deep breathing, body scanning, and focusing on the present moment. By letting go of worry and fear, they can cultivate a sense of relaxation and calmness, which may help them approach the presentation with greater confidence and focus. Over time, incorporating mindfulness into daily life can help reduce overall stress and anxiety levels, leading to greater emotional well-being and resilience.

Greater emotional regulation: Increased mindfulness

can contribute to greater emotional regulation as individuals become more aware of their emotional states and learn to respond to them in a more adaptive way. Letting go of reactivity and embracing emotional awareness can further promote emotional balance and well-being.

Let's say an employee receives negative feedback from their supervisor during a performance review. Instead of immediately reacting with anger or defensiveness, the employee takes a moment to practice mindfulness by acknowledging their emotions without judgment and observing their physical sensations. By taking a few deep breaths and refocusing their attention on the present moment, the employee can respond to the feedback more constructively and adaptively. They may ask clarifying questions, acknowledge the feedback, and create a plan for improvement, rather than becoming defensive or shutting down emotionally. Through increased mindfulness, the employee can regulate their emotional response and handle the situation in a more effective and productive manner, leading to better outcomes for both them and the company.

Improved self-awareness: Increased mindfulness can lead to improved self-awareness as individuals become more attuned to their thoughts, emotions, and physical sensations. Letting go of self-judgment and embracing self-compassion can support continued growth and self-discovery.

One example of how increased mindfulness can lead to improved self-awareness is through meditation. During meditation, individuals are encouraged to focus on their breath and observe their thoughts and emotions without judgment. By doing so, individuals can become more aware of their habitual thought patterns and emotional reactions.

Through this process of observation, individuals can develop a deeper understanding of themselves and their internal experiences. They may begin to identify patterns and triggers that contribute to their stress or emotional distress.

This increased self-awareness can lead to greater insight and the ability to make positive changes in their lives.

For example, a person who struggles with social anxiety may notice that they tend to avoid social situations or experience negative thoughts and physical sensations when in social settings. Through mindfulness practice, they may become more aware of their thoughts and sensations and learn to respond to them in a more adaptive way. They may begin to challenge their negative thoughts or engage in relaxation techniques to manage their physical symptoms. This increased self-awareness and self-regulation can lead to improved well-being and greater control over their life.

Enhanced cognitive functioning: Increased mindfulness can contribute to enhanced cognitive functioning as individuals become more focused and attentive to the present moment. Letting go of distraction and embracing concentration can further enhance mental clarity and focus.

One example of this can be seen in a student who regularly practices mindfulness meditation before studying for exams. By taking a few minutes to focus their attention and clear their mind, they are better able to concentrate on their studies and retain important information. They may find that they are able to recall more information on the exam and perform better overall.

Similarly, individuals who practice mindfulness may be better able to regulate their emotions and respond to stressful situations in a more adaptive way. This can help them stay calm and focused under pressure, which can be beneficial in many areas of life, such as work or personal relationships.

Greater appreciation for life: Increased mindfulness can lead to a greater appreciation for life as individuals become more present and engaged in the world around them. Letting go of preconceptions and embracing curiosity and wonder can promote a sense of awe and gratitude for the richness of life.

An example of this could be a person who has been feeling stressed and overwhelmed by their work and personal responsibilities. They may feel like they are constantly rushing through life, never really taking the time to appreciate the present moment. However, by practicing mindfulness, they begin to slow down and pay more attention to their surroundings. They may notice the beauty of nature during their morning commute or take time to savor the taste of their food during meals.

By letting go of distractions and embracing the present moment, they can better appreciate life's simple joys. This can lead to increased feelings of contentment and happiness.

Enhanced spiritual connection: Increased mindfulness can also contribute to enhanced spiritual connection as individuals become more attuned to their own inner wisdom and a sense of purpose. Letting go of attachment and embracing detachment and acceptance can support a deeper connection to the divine and a sense of inner peace.

An example of how mindfulness can enhance spiritual connection could be a person who regularly practices meditation and self-reflection. Through these practices, they develop a deeper understanding of their inner self and their place in the world. They may begin to see themselves as part of a greater whole, connected to all living beings and the natural world. They let go of the need to control everything and instead embrace a sense of detachment and acceptance of things as they are. This can lead to a greater sense of inner peace and feeling connected to a higher power or spiritual realm. With this enhanced spiritual connection, they may feel more grounded and purposeful in their daily life and more open to experiences of awe and wonder.

Greater sense of purpose and meaning: Increased mindfulness can lead to a greater sense of purpose and meaning in life as individuals become more aware of their values, goals, and priorities. Letting go of distraction and embracing intention and focus can promote greater clarity and direction in life.

For example, imagine someone who has been feeling lost and unsure about their career path. By practicing mindfulness and becoming more present and aware of their thoughts and emotions, they may begin to recognize their true passions and values. They may let go of external pressures and expectations and instead embrace their own unique path, leading to a greater sense of purpose and fulfillment in their work and life. Through mindfulness, they have developed a clearer understanding of their priorities and goals, allowing them to move forward with intention and focus.

Improved interpersonal relationships: Increased mindfulness can also contribute to improved interpersonal relationships as individuals become more attuned to the needs and feelings of others. Letting go of judgment and embracing compassion and empathy can promote greater connection and understanding.

Imagine a person who has been struggling to connect with their romantic partner. They decide to practice mindfulness in their interactions, becoming more aware of their own thoughts and emotions and more attentive to their partner's nonverbal cues and expressions. Through this practice, they become more empathetic and compassionate towards their partner, allowing them to build a deeper connection and understanding. This leads to greater intimacy, trust, and satisfaction in the relationship. Additionally, the individual may find that their improved mindfulness extends to other relationships in their life, such as with family, friends, and coworkers, leading to more positive and fulfilling interactions.

Enhanced physical health: Increased mindfulness can lead to enhanced physical health as individuals become more aware of their bodies and learn to respond to physical sensations in a more balanced and healthy way. Letting go of tension and embracing relaxation and mindfulness can promote physical relaxation and well-being.

One example of how increased mindfulness can enhance physical health is by helping individuals better manage chronic pain. People with chronic pain often experience anxiety and stress related to their condition, which can exacerbate their pain and make it more difficult to cope. Mindfulness practices such as meditation, deep breathing, and yoga have been shown to help individuals reduce pain-related anxiety and stress, leading to improved pain management and greater physical comfort.

For instance, a study published in the Journal of Psychosomatic Research found that individuals with chronic low back pain who participated in a mindfulness-based stress reduction program reported significant reductions in pain intensity and disability and improvements in physical functioning and quality of life. By practicing mindfulness, these individuals were able to let go of the mental and emotional tension associated with their pain and learn to respond to physical sensations in a more relaxed and accepting way.

More fulfilling and peaceful life: Increased mindfulness can lead to a more fulfilling and peaceful life as individuals learn to embrace the present moment with greater awareness, acceptance, and compassion. Letting go of attachment to the past and future and embracing the present moment can promote a sense of inner peace and well-being.

Imagine someone struggling with anxiety and constantly overwhelmed by their thoughts and emotions. Through practicing mindfulness meditation, they learn to observe their thoughts and emotions with detachment and without getting caught up in them. They also learn to focus their attention on the present moment rather than dwelling on past regrets or worrying about the future. Over time, this leads to a greater sense of inner peace and fulfillment as they learn to respond to stress and negative emotions in a more balanced and centered way. They may also experience improved physical health and greater emotional well-being as they learn to let go of tension and embrace relaxation and mindfulness.

Improved Sense of Purpose

Letting go of negative emotions and past experiences can allow us to see our lives more clearly and focus on what's truly important to us. This can lead to a greater sense of purpose and direction. We may discover new passions or pursuits that align with our values, or we may find renewed motivation to pursue existing goals. Additionally, letting go of past mistakes or regrets can free us to learn from them and use those lessons to guide us in creating a meaningful and fulfilling life.

Here are some key advantages of an improved sense of purpose in terms of enhancing inner peace, along with the associated benefits of letting go:

Reduced stress and anxiety: Having a clear sense of purpose can lead to reduced stress and anxiety, as individuals feel more confident and grounded in their decisions and direction. Letting go of doubt and indecision can further promote relaxation and calmness.

A good example of this is struggling to make a career change. They may feel uncertain about their direction and struggle with indecision, which can lead to feelings of anxiety and stress. However, if they take the time to clarify their values and goals and develop a clear sense of purpose for their career, they may feel more confident and grounded in their decision-making. They can let go of doubt and embrace their purpose, which can lead to a greater sense of calm and inner peace. As a result, they may experience reduced stress and anxiety and feel more fulfilled in their career and overall life.

Enhanced self-awareness: Having a clear sense of purpose can also lead to enhanced self-awareness, as individuals become more attuned to their own values, beliefs, and priorities. Letting go of external pressures and expectations can support continued growth and self-discovery.

Suppose a person is struggling with their career path

and feels unfulfilled in their current job. After reflecting on their values and what is important to them, they may realize that their true passion lies in a completely different field. By embracing this sense of purpose and making the necessary changes to pursue their passion, they may develop a greater sense of self-awareness and a deeper understanding of their own priorities and goals.

By letting go of external pressures and expectations, individuals can focus on what truly matters to them and develop a stronger sense of self. This can lead to increased confidence as individuals become more comfortable expressing themselves and standing up for their own beliefs and values. In turn, this enhanced self-awareness can contribute to greater personal and professional success, as individuals are able to align their actions and goals with their own unique sense of purpose.

Greater focus and motivation: Having a clear sense of purpose can contribute to greater focus and motivation, as individuals have a clear goal or direction to work towards. Letting go of distraction and procrastination can further enhance drive and productivity.

A student who wants to become a doctor is an example of how having a clear sense of purpose can lead to greater focus and motivation. With a clear sense of purpose, they are more likely to remain focused and motivated throughout their studies, despite the challenges they may face. They are less likely to become distracted by other activities or lose sight of their goal, which can contribute to procrastination and a lack of productivity. By letting go of these distractions and embracing their purpose, they can maintain their drive and work towards achieving their goal of becoming a doctor. This can lead to greater focus and motivation in their studies and ultimately contribute to their success in their chosen career.

Improved decision-making: Having a clear sense of purpose can lead to improved decision-making, as individuals are more able to assess options and align them with their values and goals. Letting go of indecision and analysis paralysis can promote confidence and assertiveness.

Imagine an individual who has been offered two job opportunities - one with a higher salary and benefits but a company culture that does not align with their values, and another with a lower salary but a more meaningful mission and positive work culture. By having a clear sense of their personal purpose and values, the individual can make a decision that aligns with their priorities rather than solely based on financial gain. They can let go of indecision and choose the job that aligns with their values and an overall sense of purpose, leading to greater fulfillment and job satisfaction.

Enhanced sense of fulfillment: Having a clear sense of purpose can contribute to an enhanced sense of fulfillment, as individuals feel that their actions and choices align with their values and goals. Letting go of external validation and embracing inner satisfaction can promote a deeper sense of well-being and contentment.

An example of how having a clear sense of purpose can enhance one's sense of fulfillment is in a career setting. Let's say an individual is working in a job that doesn't align with their values or passions, and they feel unfulfilled in their work. However, after exploring their interests and values, they discover that they have a passion for environmental sustainability. They decide to switch to a career in sustainability and work towards creating a positive impact on the environment. Doing work that aligns with their purpose makes them feel more fulfilled and satisfied in their daily work. They let go of the need for external validation or societal pressure to work in a certain industry and instead focus on the internal satisfaction that comes with doing work that aligns with their purpose. This increased sense of fulfillment can also spill over into other areas of their life, leading to a greater overall sense of well-being and contentment.

Greater resilience and adaptability: Having a clear sense of purpose can also contribute to greater resilience and adaptability, as individuals are better able to navigate challenges and setbacks with a sense of direction and purpose. Letting go of rigidity and embracing flexibility and creativity can promote greater adaptability and problem-solving.

For instance, a person who has a clear sense of purpose in becoming a lawyer may encounter academic or personal challenges that could threaten their ability to achieve their goal. However, their strong sense of purpose can motivate them to persist and find alternative ways to overcome obstacles. They may seek out additional academic resources or personal support systems to help them stay on track. By letting go of the belief that there is only one path to their goal and embracing a mindset of flexibility and creativity, they can adapt to the challenges they face and continue to work towards their purpose with resilience and determination. This can lead to greater satisfaction and a sense of accomplishment as they navigate their way toward achieving their goals.

Enhanced spiritual connection: Having a clear sense of purpose can lead to an enhanced spiritual connection, as individuals feel that their actions and choices align with their higher purpose or divine calling. Letting go of attachment to external outcomes and embracing surrender and trust can promote a deeper sense of inner peace and connection to the divine.

Let's say someone who feels called to help others may develop a sense of purpose by volunteering at a local charity or starting a non-profit organization. As they work towards this goal, they may feel a sense of spiritual fulfillment and connection to something greater than themselves. They may also encounter challenges and setbacks along the way, but by letting go of attachment to specific outcomes and trusting in the journey, they can develop a greater sense of inner peace and resilience. This can lead to a deeper sense of connection to their spiritual beliefs and a greater sense of purpose in their life.

Improved relationships: Having a clear sense of purpose can also contribute to improved relationships, as individuals are better able to communicate their values and goals with others and seek out relationships that align with their purpose. Letting go of fear and embracing vulnerability and connection can promote deeper and more fulfilling relationships.

For instance, imagine someone who values creativity and social impact. If they pursue a career in the arts, they may find more fulfillment in their work and be able to share their passion with others. They may also be able to connect with like-minded individuals who share their values and goals, which can lead to deeper and more meaningful relationships. Additionally, they may feel more comfortable being vulnerable with others about their passions and aspirations, which can lead to greater connection and understanding in their relationships.

On the other hand, if an individual feels lost or unsure of their purpose, they may struggle to find fulfillment in their work and may not be able to connect with others who share their values and goals. This can lead to feelings of isolation and disconnection in their relationships. By having a clear sense of purpose, individuals can improve their relationships by finding common ground with others and building deeper connections based on shared values and goals.

Enhanced physical health: Having a clear sense of purpose can lead to enhanced physical health, as individuals are more motivated to engage in healthy behaviors that support their goals and values. Letting go of self-destructive habits and embracing self-care and healthy living can promote physical well-being and vitality.

For example, let's say someone has a clear sense of purpose to live a healthy and active lifestyle. They may be more motivated to engage in regular exercise, eat a balanced and nutritious diet, and prioritize self-care practices such as getting enough sleep and managing stress. This dedication to their purpose can lead to a healthier body, improved immune function, and better overall physical well-being. By letting go of unhealthy habits and prioritizing healthy behaviors, they can promote long-term health and vitality.

More fulfilling and peaceful life: Having a clear sense of purpose can lead to a more fulfilling and peaceful life, as individuals are able to engage with their passions and contribute to the world in a meaningful way. Letting go of external pressures and embracing inner fulfillment and purpose can promote a sense of inner peace and well-being.

Imagine someone who has always had a passion for music but has never pursued it because they felt it wasn't a practical career choice. However, as they get older, they realize that their love for music brings them a deep sense of fulfillment and joy. They decide to take music lessons and start performing at local events. By aligning their actions with their passions, they can create a more fulfilling life and find inner peace in doing what they love. They let go of external pressures and expectations and embrace their unique sense of purpose, which brings them a greater sense of satisfaction and contentment in life.

Greater Sense of Gratitude

When we let go of negative emotions, we can focus more on the positive aspects of our lives. This can help us develop a greater sense of gratitude for the good things we have, whether it's our health, our relationships, or our job. Instead of taking these things for granted, we can fully appreciate them and find joy in our everyday experiences. Cultivating gratitude can also help us maintain a positive attitude even when things get tough and help us build resilience in the face of challenges.

Here are some key advantages of a greater sense of gratitude in terms of promoting inner peace, along with the associated benefits of letting go:

Reduced stress and anxiety: A greater sense of gratitude can lead to reduced stress and anxiety, as individuals are better able to focus on the positive aspects of their lives and find peace in the present moment. Letting go of attachment to old patterns of stress and worry and embracing new ways of gratitude and positive thinking can promote greater inner peace and reduced stress and anxiety.

An example of how gratitude can reduce stress and anxiety is a daily gratitude practice. This could involve taking a few moments each day to reflect on things in your life that you are grateful for, such as loved ones, good health, a comfortable home, or a fulfilling job. By focusing on the positive aspects of your life, even in the midst of stress or difficult circumstances, you can shift your mindset from one of stress and worry to one of gratitude and appreciation.

Imagine someone who has a demanding job and is feeling stressed and overwhelmed. They decide to start a daily gratitude practice by writing down three things they are grateful for each morning before starting work. Over time, they begin to notice that they are better able to manage their stress and anxiety, even during challenging times at work. They start to focus more on the positive aspects of their job, such as the sense of accomplishment they feel when they complete a project or the supportive relationships they have with their colleagues. By cultivating gratitude, they can shift their mindset from one of stress and anxiety to one of gratitude and positivity, leading to a more fulfilling and peaceful life.

Improved mental health: A greater sense of gratitude can also contribute to improved mental health, as individuals are better able to cultivate a positive outlook and find joy in their daily lives. Letting go of attachment to negative thoughts and beliefs and embracing new ways of gratitude and positive thinking can promote improved mental health and greater inner peace.

One example of how gratitude can contribute to improved mental health is in the case of a person who has struggled with depression. By practicing gratitude on a regular basis, such as by keeping a gratitude journal or regularly expressing gratitude towards others, they may be able to shift their focus away from negative thoughts and emotions and toward the positive aspects of their life. This can help to improve their mood, increase their sense of well-being, and reduce symptoms of depression.

For instance, the person may write down three things they are grateful for each day: a supportive friend, a comfortable home, or a beautiful sunset. By actively seeking out and acknowledging the positive aspects of their life, they can begin to reframe their mindset toward positivity and optimism. This may not only improve their mental health but also enhance their overall quality of life.

Enhanced relationships: A greater sense of gratitude can also contribute to enhanced relationships, as individuals are better able to appreciate and express gratitude for the people in their lives. Letting go of attachment to old patterns of conflict and negativity and embracing new ways of gratitude and positivity in relationships can promote greater inner peace and improved relationships.

For example, a couple may have been struggling with a pattern of negative communication and criticism towards each other. By cultivating a greater sense of gratitude for each other's positive qualities and actions, they can shift the tone of their interactions and promote more positive and supportive communication. They may start to express gratitude for small gestures and actions, such as cooking a meal or doing the laundry, and acknowledge each other's efforts and strengths. By letting go of old patterns of negativity and embracing new ways of gratitude and positivity, they can promote greater intimacy and harmony in their relationship.

Improved physical health: A greater sense of gratitude can lead to improved physical health, as individuals are better able to engage in healthy lifestyle habits such as regular exercise, healthy eating, and stress management. Letting go of attachment to old patterns of stress and anxiety and embracing new ways of gratitude and self-care can promote improved physical health and greater inner peace.

For example, someone who practices gratitude may start each day by expressing gratitude for their health and committing to taking care of their body. They may take time to prepare healthy meals and prioritize regular exercise, knowing that these actions support their physical health and overall well-being. Additionally, by letting go of stress and anxiety and embracing gratitude and self-care, they may experience better sleep, reduced inflammation, and a stronger immune system, all of which contribute to improved physical health. Overall, a greater sense of gratitude can promote a healthier lifestyle and greater physical well-being.

Improved sense of purpose: A greater sense of gratitude can also contribute to an improved sense of purpose, as individuals are better able to find meaning and fulfillment in their lives. Letting go of attachment to old patterns of negativity and self-doubt and embracing new ways of gratitude and positivity can promote an improved sense of purpose and greater inner peace.

Let's say a person may have been feeling unfulfilled and uncertain about their career path. However, by practicing gratitude and focusing on the positive aspects of their current job or the opportunities it provides, they may begin to feel more content and purposeful. They may also start to explore new avenues for growth and development, such as taking on new challenges at work or pursuing hobbies and interests outside of work. By letting go of negative thoughts and embracing gratitude, they can find greater meaning and fulfillment in their life's journey.

By incorporating the practice of letting go and focusing on a greater sense of gratitude, individuals can experience numerous benefits for promoting inner peace, fostering personal growth and self-awareness, and improving overall well-being.

CHAPTER 6 - SPACE FOR NEW OPPORTUNITIES

Letting go can be a difficult and painful process, but it's also essential for personal growth and transformation. One of the most significant benefits of letting go is creating space for new opportunities in our lives. Holding onto something, whether it's a job, a relationship, or an idea, can take up mental and emotional space that could be used for something else. Letting go can help us release that mental and emotional burden and make room for new possibilities and experiences to come into our lives.

In this chapter, we'll explore some of the specific benefits of letting go and creating space for new opportunities.

Room for Growth

Letting go of old habits, thought patterns, and beliefs can be challenging, but it can also be incredibly liberating. When we're willing to let go of what no longer serves us, we make room for new possibilities and opportunities. We create space for growth and self-discovery and become more open to new ideas and experiences.

For example, if we're always sticking to the same routine, we may not have the chance to try new things or explore new interests. But when we let go of that routine and try something different, we may discover a new passion or talent that we never knew existed. Similarly, if we're always holding onto a particular belief or viewpoint, we may not be open to seeing things from a different perspective. Letting go of that belief can open our minds to new ideas and ways of thinking.

Letting go can also be a catalyst for personal growth. When we release old patterns and beliefs, we create space for new learning and self-discovery. We can explore our values and passions more deeply, and we may discover new aspects of ourselves that we never knew existed. This can be a powerful way to transform our lives and create a greater sense of purpose and fulfillment.

Here are some key advantages of creating room for growth in terms of enhancing space for new opportunities, along with the associated benefits of letting go:

Increased creativity: Creating room for growth can lead to increased creativity, as individuals are more open to exploring new ideas and approaches. Letting go of limiting beliefs and old habits can further promote innovation and creativity.

For example, a graphic designer who feels that their work has become stagnant may choose to create room for growth by attending design conferences, exploring new design software or tools, or collaborating with other designers. By embracing new ideas and approaches and letting go of limiting beliefs such as "I'm not good enough" or "I'm not creative enough," the designer can tap into their creativity and produce innovative designs that stand out. As they continue to explore and experiment, they may find that their work becomes more exciting and fulfilling, leading to increased creativity and professional growth.

Enhanced learning and development: Creating room for growth can contribute to enhanced learning and development, as individuals are more receptive to feedback and new experiences. Letting go of defensiveness and embracing openness and curiosity can support continued growth and learning.

For example, a student who is struggling in a particular subject may create room for growth by seeking out additional resources or reaching out to their teacher for extra help. By letting go of their fear of failure and embracing a growth mindset, they become more open to learning and development. This newfound openness allows them to be more receptive to feedback from their teacher and to explore new approaches to learning the subject matter. As a result, they may find that their grades improve and their understanding deepens, leading to a greater sense of accomplishment and confidence in their academic abilities. By embracing a growth and development mindset, individuals can create room for continued learning and self-improvement.

Greater adaptability: Creating room for growth can also contribute to greater adaptability, as individuals are better able to navigate change and uncertainty. Letting go of rigidity and embracing flexibility and resilience can promote greater adaptability and problem-solving.

For example, imagine an employee who has been working in the same role for several years and has become comfortable with their routine. However, their company introduces new technology and processes that require them to adapt and learn new skills. By creating room for growth and being open to learning, the employee is able to embrace changes and adapt quickly. They let go of their old habits and routines and embrace the opportunity to develop new skills and approaches. As a result, they can contribute more to the company and feel more confident in their ability to navigate future changes and challenges.

Improved decision-making: Creating room for growth can lead to improved decision-making, as individuals are better able to assess options and consider new possibilities. Letting go of attachment to old ways of thinking and embracing curiosity and exploration can promote better decision-making.

For example, a person who has been working in the same job for many years may feel stagnant and unfulfilled. By creating room for growth, they may decide to explore new career options and consider the possibilities of pursuing a different path. By letting go of attachment to their current job and embracing curiosity and exploration, they may discover a new field that aligns more with their passions and values. This process of creating room for growth can lead to improved decision-making, as they are better able to assess their options and consider new possibilities, ultimately leading to a more fulfilling and satisfying career path.

Greater sense of purpose: Creating room for growth can also contribute to a greater sense of purpose, as individuals are able to explore new possibilities and align their actions with their values and goals. Letting go of limiting beliefs and embracing possibility and potential can promote a sense of inner fulfillment and purpose.

For example, an employee who actively seeks out feedback from their colleagues and supervisor and is open to learning and improving their communication skills is more likely to develop stronger relationships with their colleagues and excel in their role. This growth mindset can also benefit personal relationships, as individuals become more receptive to feedback and better equipped to communicate their needs and concerns.

Enhanced confidence and self-esteem: Creating room for growth can lead to enhanced confidence and self-esteem as individuals take on new challenges and learn new skills. Letting go of self-doubt and embracing self-acceptance and self-love can support continued growth and development.

For example, imagine someone who has always wanted to learn how to play an instrument but has never had the opportunity to do so. By creating room for growth and exploring this interest, they enroll in music lessons and begin to develop their skills. As they learn and improve, they gain a sense of confidence in their abilities and a greater appreciation for themselves. They let go of self-doubt and limiting beliefs about their abilities and embrace self-acceptance and self-love. This newfound confidence and self-esteem can extend beyond their musical pursuits and positively impact other areas of their life.

Improved relationships: Creating room for growth can also contribute to improved relationships, as individuals are better able to communicate their needs and boundaries and seek out relationships that align with their values and goals. Letting go of toxic relationships and embracing healthy connections can promote deeper and more fulfilling relationships.

For example, a person who wants to grow and develop in their relationships may decide to work on their communication skills and set boundaries to improve the quality of their relationships. By creating space for growth and taking proactive steps to improve their relationships, they may be able to cultivate deeper connections with their loved ones, build trust and understanding, and enjoy more fulfilling relationships. Letting go of negative patterns and behaviors that harm relationships and embracing new healthy relationship patterns can lead to better communication, trust, and a sense of closeness.

Greater sense of fulfillment: Creating room for growth can lead to greater fulfillment as individuals engage in activities and pursuits that bring them joy and meaning. Letting go of old habits and patterns and embracing new possibilities and experiences can promote a sense of inner peace and contentment.

For example, let's say someone has always had a passion for writing, but due to various circumstances, they have never pursued it seriously. By creating room for growth and allowing themselves to explore their passion, they may take writing classes, start a blog, or join a writing group. As they engage in these activities and pursue their passion, they may feel a greater sense of fulfillment and joy as they are doing something that aligns with their values and brings them meaning. By letting go of old patterns and embracing new possibilities, individuals can create a more fulfilling and satisfying life for themselves.

Enhanced physical health: Creating room for growth can also lead to enhanced physical health, as individuals engage in healthy behaviors and activities that support their well-being. Letting go of self-destructive habits and embracing self-care and healthy living can promote physical well-being and vitality.

For example, a person who wants to create room for growth in their physical health may start by setting a goal to exercise for at least 30 minutes a day. As they begin to prioritize exercise and create a routine, they may also start to explore other healthy habits, such as eating a balanced diet and practicing stress-management techniques like yoga or meditation. By letting go of old habits that may have been detrimental to their physical health and embracing new ways of self-care and healthy living, they can promote physical well-being and vitality, leading to a more fulfilling and energized life.

More fulfilling and abundant life: Creating room for growth can lead to a more fulfilling and abundant life as individuals open themselves up to new experiences and possibilities. Letting go of fear and embracing courage and possibility can promote a sense of adventure and excitement for life.

For example, someone who has always dreamed of traveling but has held back due to fear or financial constraints may decide to take the leap and plan a trip. Opening themselves up to this new experience and letting go of limiting beliefs can expand their horizons and create new memories and connections. This sense of adventure and fulfillment can also bring a sense of abundance as they realize the richness and diversity of the world around them. By creating room for growth and embracing new experiences, individuals can create a more fulfilling and abundant life for themselves.

By incorporating the practice of letting go and focusing on creating room for growth, individuals can experience numerous benefits for creating space for new opportunities, promoting personal growth and self-awareness, and fostering a sense of inner peace and well-being.

Increased Creativity

When we're holding onto old ideas and beliefs, it can limit our thinking and creativity. Letting go can help us break free from those limitations and think outside the box. We can approach problems from new angles and come up with unique solutions. This can be especially helpful in our personal and professional lives, as it allows us to be more innovative and stand out from the crowd.

Letting go can also help us tap into our own unique creativity. When past experiences or negative emotions do not weigh us down, we're more able to access our own creative potential. This can lead to greater fulfillment and a sense of purpose in our lives.

Overall, letting go can create space for new ideas, experiences, and opportunities that can lead to personal growth and transformation. It can help us tap into our creativity and approach life from a more open-minded perspective.

Here are some key advantages of increased creativity in terms of enhancing space for new opportunities, along with the associated benefits of letting go:

Enhanced problem-solving: Increased creativity can lead to enhanced problem-solving, as individuals are more open to exploring new ideas and approaches. Letting go of old patterns and habits can further promote innovative problem-solving.

For example, a team working on a project may feel stuck and unable to come up with a solution to a particular problem. By creating room for growth and allowing for a more creative and open-minded approach, they may be able to generate new ideas and solutions to the problem at hand. This could involve brainstorming sessions or bringing in outside perspectives to provide fresh insights. By letting go of rigid ways of thinking and embracing creativity and innovation, the team can enhance their problem-solving skills and find a successful resolution to their challenges.

Greater adaptability: Increased creativity can also contribute to greater adaptability, as individuals are better able to navigate change and uncertainty. Letting go of rigidity and embracing flexibility and resilience can promote greater adaptability and openness to new ideas.

For example, a company that fosters a culture of creativity may be better equipped to adapt to changes in the market or industry. By encouraging employees to think outside the box and try new approaches, the company is better able to navigate challenges and identify opportunities for growth. This increased adaptability can help the company stay ahead of the competition and thrive in a rapidly changing business environment. Additionally, by letting go of rigid thinking and embracing flexibility and openness, employees may feel more empowered and engaged in their work, leading to greater job satisfaction and productivity.

Improved decision-making: Increased creativity can lead to improved decision-making, as individuals are better able to assess options and consider new possibilities. Letting go of attachment to old ways of thinking and embracing curiosity and exploration can promote better decision-making.

For example, a marketing team looking to develop a new campaign may use creativity to come up with new and innovative ideas. By thinking outside the box and considering unconventional approaches, they may be able to create a campaign that stands out from competitors and resonates with their target audience. This creative thinking can also lead to improved decision-making as they assess and choose the best approach for the campaign, considering all available options and their potential impact. Letting go of attachment to old ways of thinking and embracing curiosity and exploration can promote a culture of creative thinking and better decision-making within the team.

Greater innovation: Increased creativity can also contribute to greater innovation, as individuals are more willing to take risks and explore new territory. Letting go of the fear of failure and embracing a sense of play and experimentation can promote greater innovation and breakthroughs.

For example, a tech company encourages its employees to engage in regular brainstorming sessions to generate new ideas for products and services. By creating a space for creativity and experimentation, employees feel free to explore new ideas without the fear of failure or judgment. This openness to new possibilities and willingness to take risks can lead to greater innovation and breakthroughs in the company's offerings, ultimately driving growth and success. By letting go of rigid thinking and embracing creativity and play, the company can stay at the forefront of its industry and deliver unique and valuable solutions to its customers.

Enhanced self-expression: Increased creativity can also contribute to enhanced self-expression, as individuals have more tools and resources to express themselves in unique and meaningful ways. Letting go of self-doubt and embracing a sense of authenticity and vulnerability can promote greater self-expression and creative fulfillment.

For example, someone who has always enjoyed writing but has been hesitant to share their work with others due to fear of criticism or rejection may begin to experiment with different writing styles and techniques. By exploring their creativity and taking risks with their writing, they may discover a new passion for self-expression and feel more confident in sharing their work with others. By letting go of self-doubt and embracing vulnerability, they can tap into their authentic voice and experience greater creative fulfillment. This enhanced self-expression can also bring a sense of joy and fulfillment to their daily life as they engage with their creativity in a meaningful and fulfilling way.

Improved relationships: Increased creativity can also contribute to improved relationships, as individuals are better able to communicate their needs and emotions in creative and innovative ways. Letting go of old patterns of communication and embracing new ways of expression can promote deeper and more fulfilling relationships.

For example, let's say that a couple is struggling to communicate effectively in their relationship. By exploring new creative approaches to communication, such as writing letters or creating art together, they can express their feelings more authentically and meaningfully. This new approach to communication can help them better understand each other's needs and emotions, leading to a deeper and more fulfilling relationship. By letting go of old patterns of communication and embracing new ways of expression, individuals can improve their relationships and enhance their overall well-being.

Greater sense of purpose: Increased creativity can lead to greater purpose as individuals engage in activities and pursuits that align with their values and goals. Letting go of limiting beliefs and embracing possibility and potential can promote a sense of inner fulfillment and purpose.

For example, someone who values social justice may use their creativity to raise awareness and funds for a cause they are passionate about. By using their skills and talents to contribute to something greater than themselves, they may find a greater sense of purpose and fulfillment in their life. This sense of purpose can also inspire continued creativity and innovation as they seek new and creative ways to impact the world around them positively.

Enhanced personal growth: Increased creativity can also contribute to enhanced personal growth as individuals engage in activities that challenge and expand their skills and abilities. Letting go of self-limiting beliefs and embracing a growth mindset can support continued personal growth and development.

For example, a person who has always been interested in painting but has never tried it may decide to take a painting class. Through this creative pursuit, they may discover new skills and abilities that they didn't know they had. They may also encounter challenges that push them to grow and develop their artistic abilities further. By letting go of self-doubt and embracing the process of learning and growth, they can experience enhanced personal growth and fulfillment.

Greater sense of fulfillment: Increased creativity can lead to greater fulfillment as individuals engage in activities and pursuits that bring them joy and meaning. Letting go of old habits and patterns and embracing new possibilities and experiences can promote a sense of inner peace and contentment.

For example, someone who enjoys cooking may find a sense of fulfillment and creativity in experimenting with new ingredients and flavors, creating unique dishes, and presenting them in visually appealing ways. Through this process, they can let go of old habits and patterns in their cooking and embrace new possibilities and experiences, leading to a greater sense of inner peace and contentment.

More fulfilling and abundant life: Increased creativity can lead to a more fulfilling and abundant life as individuals open themselves up to new experiences and possibilities. Letting go of fear and embracing courage and possibility can promote a sense of adventure and excitement for life.

For example, an individual who wants to increase their creativity and sense of adventure may decide to try a new hobby or travel to a new place. They may choose to take up photography and explore new and exciting locations to capture stunning images. By stepping out of their comfort zone and trying new things, they open themselves up to a more fulfilling and abundant life filled with new experiences and opportunities. Letting go of fear and embracing courage can allow them to push beyond their limits and explore new possibilities they never thought possible, leading to a life rich with excitement and adventure.

By incorporating the practice of letting go and focusing on increasing creativity, individuals can experience numerous benefits for creating space for new opportunities, promoting personal growth and self-awareness, and fostering a sense of inner peace and well-being.

New Experiences

Letting go can create space for new experiences in our lives that can lead to personal growth and a more fulfilling life. When we hold onto old patterns or habits, we may miss out on opportunities that could bring us joy or help us discover new passions. Letting go allows us to open ourselves up to new experiences that may broaden our horizons and help us find new interests or passions. It can also be a chance to take risks and try things we may have been too afraid to do before. By doing so, we may discover new strengths or abilities we never knew we had, which can lead to greater self-awareness and self-confidence.

Here are some key advantages of new experiences in terms of enhancing space for new opportunities, along with the associated benefits of letting go:

Enhanced personal growth: New experiences can contribute to enhanced personal growth as individuals challenge themselves and expand their skills and abilities. Letting go of the fear of failure and embracing a growth mindset can support continued personal growth and development.

For example, someone who has always been interested in public speaking but has been too afraid to try it may take a public speaking course or join a Toastmasters group. They can develop greater confidence and communication abilities by challenging themselves to step out of their comfort zone and expand their skills. This new experience can also lead to other opportunities and personal growth in areas they never imagined, such as leadership or mentorship. By letting go of their fear of failure and embracing a growth mindset, individuals can achieve personal growth and development that enhances their life and opens new possibilities.

Greater adaptability: New experiences can also contribute to greater adaptability, as individuals are exposed to new situations and challenges. Letting go of rigidity and embracing flexibility and resilience can promote greater adaptability and openness to new experiences.

For example, someone who has always lived in the same town may decide to travel to a new country for the first time. This new experience can expose them to different cultures, languages, and ways of life, which can challenge their perspective and expand their worldview. By letting go of their fear of the unknown and embracing the new experience with curiosity and openness, they can develop greater adaptability and resilience in navigating new situations and challenges in the future.

Improved problem-solving: New experiences can also lead to improved problem-solving, as individuals are exposed to new situations that require creative solutions. Letting go of old patterns and habits can further promote innovative problem-solving.

For example, a person who has always worked in an office environment may decide to take on a new job in a completely different industry, such as healthcare. In this new role, they are faced with challenges and problems they have never encountered before, such as navigating complex medical systems or communicating with patients with different needs and backgrounds. Through this new experience, they develop new problem-solving skills and approaches and learn to think outside the box to find creative solutions. This newfound ability to tackle complex problems and think creatively can then be applied in other areas of their life as well, leading to improved problem-solving skills overall.

Increased confidence: New experiences can also contribute to increased confidence as individuals take on new challenges and succeed in new endeavors. Letting go of self-doubt and embracing self-acceptance and self-love can support continued confidence and self-assurance.

For example, trying a new hobby, such as learning a new

language, can be a new experience that contributes to personal growth. It challenges individuals to expand their knowledge and skill set in a different area, which can improve cognitive function and increase confidence. Letting go of the fear of making mistakes and embracing the process of learning can further promote personal growth and skill development.

Greater sense of purpose: New experiences can lead to a greater sense of purpose as individuals engage in activities and pursuits that align with their values and goals. Letting go of limiting beliefs and embracing possibility and potential can promote a sense of inner fulfillment and purpose.

For example, someone who has always been interested in helping animals but has never pursued it may decide to volunteer at a local animal shelter or take up a job in an animal welfare organization. By aligning their actions with their values and passions, they can lead a more purposeful life and positively impact the world around them. This sense of purpose and fulfillment can also bring a sense of inner peace and contentment, as they feel that they are living a meaningful life that is in line with their personal values and beliefs. By letting go of the pressure to conform to external expectations and embracing their unique sense of purpose, individuals can create a more fulfilling and peaceful life for themselves.

Improved decision-making: New experiences can lead to improved decision-making, as individuals are exposed to new information and perspectives that inform their choices. Letting go of attachment to old ways of thinking and embracing curiosity and exploration can promote better decision-making.

For example, a person who has only worked in one industry for their entire career may make decisions based solely on their knowledge and experience in that field. However, if they decide to take on a new job in a different industry or even travel to a new country, they will be exposed to new information, perspectives, and ways of thinking that can inform their decision-making. By letting go of attachment to old ways of thinking and embracing curiosity and exploration, they can expand their perspective and make more informed decisions. This can ultimately lead to better outcomes for themselves and those around them.

Enhanced creativity: New experiences can also contribute to enhanced creativity, as individuals are exposed to new ideas and perspectives. Letting go of old patterns of thinking and embracing a sense of play and experimentation can promote greater creativity and innovation.

For example, a person who has only ever written prose may decide to take a poetry workshop. The new experience of learning to write in a different style and form can expose them to new ideas, techniques, and perspectives that they can incorporate into their own writing. They may begin to experiment with language and imagery in new ways, leading to greater creativity and innovation in their writing. By letting go of their attachment to their old writing patterns and embracing new possibilities and experiences, they can expand their creativity and produce more unique and exciting work.

More fulfilling and abundant life: New experiences can lead to a more fulfilling and abundant life, as individuals open themselves up to new opportunities and possibilities. Letting go of fear and embracing courage and possibility can promote a sense of adventure and excitement for life.

For instance, someone who has never traveled to another country may have preconceived notions about the people and culture there. By traveling and experiencing the culture firsthand, they can gain a deeper understanding of the people and their way of life. This can lead to improved empathy and a greater appreciation for cultural diversity. The person may also be more open to learning about other cultures in the future and be more inclined to form meaningful connections with people from diverse backgrounds.

Greater sense of empathy: New experiences can also contribute to greater empathy, as individuals are exposed to new perspectives and ways of life. Letting go of judgment and embracing compassion and understanding can promote greater empathy and connection with others.

For example, volunteering at a local homeless shelter can expose individuals to the experiences and perspectives of those who are struggling with housing insecurity. By interacting with and learning from individuals in these circumstances, individuals may gain a deeper understanding and appreciation for the challenges and struggles faced by homeless individuals. This can lead to greater empathy and connection with others as individuals let go of judgment and embrace compassion and understanding.

Improved relationships: New experiences can also contribute to improved relationships, as individuals have new opportunities to connect with others and share experiences. Letting go of old patterns of communication and embracing new ways of expression can promote deeper and more fulfilling relationships.

For example, let's say someone who has always been reserved and introverted decides to try a new hobby that involves joining a group or team activity. Through this new experience, they meet new people who share their interests and passions, and they find themselves connecting with others in a way that they never had before. They let go of their old patterns of isolation and embrace new ways of communication and connection, which in turn leads to improved relationships and a greater sense of community. By allowing themselves to be open to new experiences and stepping out of their comfort zone, they can enhance their relationships and overall sense of well-being.

By incorporating the practice of letting go and focusing on new experiences, individuals can experience numerous benefits for creating space for new opportunities, promoting personal growth and self-awareness, and fostering a sense of inner peace and well-being.

Improved Decision-Making

When we let go of the need to control every outcome, we open ourselves up to a more intuitive decision-making process. Instead of making decisions based on what we "should" do or what others expect of us, we can tap into our inner wisdom and make choices that feel authentic and aligned with our values. This can lead to a greater sense of self-trust and confidence in our decision-making abilities. We may also find that we're able to make decisions more quickly and efficiently when we're not weighed down by attachment to a particular outcome. Overall, letting go can help us make better, more informed decisions that serve our highest good.

Here are some key advantages of improved decision-making in terms of enhancing space for new opportunities, along with the associated benefits of letting go:

Increased clarity: Improved decision-making can lead to increased clarity, as individuals are better able to assess their options and make informed choices. Letting go of indecision and embracing a sense of self-trust and confidence can promote greater clarity in decision-making.

For example, imagine someone struggling to make a career change but indecisive about which direction to take. By letting go of self-doubt and fear of making the wrong choice and instead embracing a growth mindset and a willingness to explore different options, they can approach the decision with greater clarity and confidence. They might research different career paths, seek advice from mentors or peers, or even try out different jobs or internships to gain hands-on experience. By taking action and trusting their own judgment, they can make a decision that aligns with their values and goals, ultimately leading to greater clarity and direction in their career.

Greater sense of control: Improved decision-making can also contribute to a greater sense of control, as individuals feel more empowered to shape their own lives. Letting go of a sense of victimhood and embracing a sense of personal responsibility can promote greater agency and control in decision-making.

For example, imagine someone struggling with financial management and feeling overwhelmed by debt. They may have a pattern of avoiding the issue or relying on others to manage their finances for them. However, by deciding to take control of their finances and seeking out resources such as financial education classes or working with a financial advisor, they can make informed decisions about their money and take action to pay off their debts. This newfound sense of control and agency can lead to a greater sense of confidence and empowerment in other areas of their life as well. By letting go of a victim mentality and embracing personal responsibility, they can shape their own financial future and feel more in control of their overall well-being.

Enhanced problem-solving: Improved decision-making can also lead to enhanced problem-solving, as individuals are better able to identify solutions and make strategic choices. Letting go of attachment to old ways of thinking and embracing curiosity and exploration can promote more innovative problem-solving.

For example, imagine a business owner who needs to decide to expand their product line. They have historically relied on a narrow range of products, but with changing market conditions, they are considering expanding into new areas. By using improved decision-making skills, the business owner can assess each option's potential risks and benefits and make a strategic choice that aligns with their overall business goals. This process of evaluating options and making informed decisions can also lead to enhanced problem-solving skills as the business owner becomes more adept at identifying solutions to challenges that arise in their business.

Improved outcomes: Improved decision-making can also

lead to improved outcomes, as individuals make more aligned choices with their goals and values. Letting go of limiting beliefs and old thinking patterns can promote better decision-making and outcomes.

For example, a person may have a long-term goal of starting their own business but may have been held back by limiting beliefs such as "I don't have enough experience" or "I don't have enough money." By improving their decision-making skills, they may be able to identify the steps needed to achieve their goal, such as taking courses or seeking out a business mentor. They may also make choices that are more aligned with their values, such as choosing to prioritize sustainability in their business practices. Ultimately, by letting go of limiting beliefs and old patterns of thinking, they may be able to make choices that lead to a more successful and fulfilling outcome.

Greater confidence: Improved decision-making can also contribute to greater confidence as individuals learn to trust their own judgment and make choices that support their well-being. Letting go of self-doubt and embracing self-acceptance and self-love can support continued confidence and self-assurance.

For example, a person who has struggled with making decisions in the past may have felt uncertain and hesitant when faced with important choices. However, as they develop their decision-making skills and make more informed and aligned choices, they may feel greater confidence in their ability to navigate life's challenges. This increased confidence can positively impact their overall well-being, as they feel more in control and empowered to make choices that support their goals and values.

Greater sense of purpose: Improved decision-making can lead to a greater sense of purpose as individuals make choices that align with their values and goals. Letting go of fear and embracing possibility and potential can promote a sense of inner fulfillment and purpose.

An example of this could be a person who has always dreamed of starting their own business but has been held back by fear of failure. Through improved decision-making, they start taking steps toward their goal, such as conducting market research, creating a business plan, and securing funding. As they make more informed and confident choices, they feel a greater sense of purpose and fulfillment as they work towards building a business that aligns with their values and goals.

Improved relationships: Improved decision-making can also contribute to improved relationships, as individuals make choices that support their own well-being and the well-being of others. Letting go of old patterns of communication and embracing new ways of expression can promote deeper and more fulfilling relationships.

For example, imagine someone who has consistently put their needs aside to please others in their relationships. Through improved decision-making, this person learns to prioritize their own well-being and make choices that support their own needs while still being considerate of others. As a result, they may experience more balanced and fulfilling relationships where they feel respected and valued. This can lead to stronger connections and a greater sense of trust and intimacy in their relationships.

Greater adaptability: Improved decision-making can also contribute to greater adaptability as individuals learn to make choices that are responsive to changing circumstances. Letting go of rigidity and embracing flexibility and resilience can promote greater adaptability and openness to new experiences.

For example, a business owner who makes strategic decisions based on market trends and consumer needs is more adaptable to changes in the industry. They may choose to diversify their product offerings or pivot their business model to serve their customers better, which can lead to long-term success and sustainability. By letting go of rigid thinking and embracing flexibility and adaptability, the business owner can make better decisions and navigate through uncertainty more easily and confidently.

More fulfilling and abundant life: Improved decision-making can lead to a more fulfilling and abundant life, as individuals make choices that support their own growth and well-being. Letting go of fear and embracing courage and possibility can promote a sense of adventure and excitement for life.

For example, a person may decide to leave their unfulfilling job and pursue a new career path that aligns with their passions and values. By making this decision, they are taking a step towards a more fulfilling and abundant life, as they are no longer settling for a job that doesn't bring them joy and satisfaction. They may experience new challenges and opportunities, but by letting go of fear and embracing courage and possibility, they can find excitement and fulfillment in their new career path.

By incorporating the practice of letting go and focusing on improved decision-making, individuals can experience numerous benefits for creating space for new opportunities, promoting personal growth and self-awareness, and fostering a sense of inner peace and well-being.

Greater Sense of Adventure

When we let go, we become more willing to step outside of our comfort zones and try new things. This can lead to a greater sense of adventure and excitement as we explore uncharted territory. We may take risks and try new activities that we may have otherwise shied away from. This can lead to new discoveries about ourselves and the world around us. And even if we fail in our new endeavors, we can still learn valuable lessons and gain a sense of accomplishment from having tried something new. Ultimately, letting go can help us embrace the unknown and find joy in the journey.

Here are some key advantages of a greater sense of adventure in terms of enhancing space for new opportunities, along with the associated benefits of letting go:

Enhanced creativity: A greater sense of adventure can contribute to enhanced creativity, as individuals are more open to exploring new ideas and perspectives. Letting go of old patterns of thinking and embracing a sense of play and experimentation can promote greater creativity and innovation.

For example, an artist who has been working in a certain style for many years may feel creatively stagnant and uninspired. However, by taking a risk and experimenting with a new medium or style, they may discover new techniques and ideas that invigorate their work and spark their creativity. By letting go of the fear of failure and embracing a sense of play and experimentation, they may create something truly unique and innovative.

Increased confidence: A greater sense of adventure can also contribute to increased confidence as individuals take risks and step outside their comfort zones. Letting go of fear and embracing a sense of self-trust and courage can support continued confidence and self-assurance.

For example, someone who has always wanted to try

skydiving but has been afraid of heights may decide to take the leap and try it out. Even though it is outside their comfort zone and may be scary, the act of taking on the challenge and conquering their fear can boost their confidence and self-assurance. They may feel more capable and willing to take on other challenges and risks in the future, leading to a greater sense of confidence and adventure in their life.

Improved decision-making: A greater sense of adventure can lead to improved decision-making, as individuals are more willing to explore new possibilities and take calculated risks. Letting go of attachment to old ways of thinking and embracing curiosity and exploration can promote better decision-making.

For example, a person who has always worked in the corporate world may feel stuck in their career and unsure of their next steps. However, if they embrace a sense of adventure and explore other options, such as starting their own business or pursuing a passion project, they may make the decision to leave their corporate job for a more fulfilling and satisfying path. By taking calculated risks and letting go of their attachment to the traditional career path, they can make a more informed and confident decision about their future.

Greater sense of purpose: A greater sense of adventure can also contribute to a greater sense of purpose as individuals engage in activities and pursuits that bring them joy and meaning. Letting go of limiting beliefs and embracing possibility and potential can promote a sense of inner fulfillment and purpose.

For many years, Sarah felt stuck in her career as a lawyer. She had always wanted to be a writer, but fear and self-doubt held her back from pursuing this passion. One day, she decided to take a writing class and was surprised by how much she enjoyed it. She began to write in her free time and eventually started submitting her work to literary journals. Though she faced rejection at first, she didn't give up and eventually got published. Through this experience, Sarah discovered a newfound sense of purpose and fulfillment, realizing that writing was her true passion all along. By embracing her sense of adventure and letting go of her limiting beliefs, she was able to create a more purposeful and fulfilling life for herself.

More fulfilling and abundant life: A greater sense of adventure can lead to a more fulfilling and abundant life as individuals open themselves up to new experiences and possibilities. Letting go of fear and embracing courage and possibility can promote a sense of excitement and fulfillment in life.

Becoming a parent can be a challenging and overwhelming experience. However, embracing a sense of adventure and being open to new ways of parenting can lead to a more fulfilling and abundant life. Letting go of the fear of making mistakes and embracing the courage to try new things can promote a sense of excitement and growth as a parent. For example, trying new activities with your children, such as camping or hiking, can create lasting memories and foster a sense of exploration and adventure.

Improved relationships: A greater sense of adventure can also contribute to improved relationships, as individuals have new opportunities to connect with others and share experiences. Letting go of old patterns of communication and embracing new ways of expression can promote deeper and more fulfilling relationships.

For example, a couple may decide to take a dance class together as a new and exciting activity. In the process of learning something new, they may develop a greater sense of trust and communication with each other. They may also discover new aspects of each other's personalities and interests, leading to a deeper connection and understanding in their relationship.

Greater adaptability: A greater sense of adventure can also contribute to greater adaptability, as individuals are exposed to new situations and challenges. Letting go of rigidity and embracing flexibility and resilience can promote greater adaptability and openness to new experiences.

For example, a person who has always lived in one place and is used to a certain way of life may feel anxious about moving to a new city for work. However, if they embrace a sense of adventure and approach the move as an opportunity to learn and grow, they may be more open to new experiences and adapt more easily to their new environment. They may be more willing to try new foods, meet new people, and explore new places, which can help them adjust to their new surroundings and thrive in their new homes.

Enhanced personal growth: A greater sense of adventure can contribute to enhanced personal growth as individuals engage in activities that challenge and expand their skills and abilities. Letting go of self-limiting beliefs and embracing a growth mindset can support continued personal growth and development.

Pursuing a hobby like gardening can contribute to enhanced personal growth as individuals engage in an activity that requires patience, persistence, and learning new skills. Letting go of self-limiting beliefs about one's abilities and embracing a growth mindset can support continued personal growth and development in the realm of gardening. As individuals learn to nurture plants and create beautiful outdoor spaces, they may also develop a deeper appreciation for the natural world and a greater sense of connection to the environment.

Improved problem-solving: A greater sense of adventure can also lead to improved problem-solving, as individuals are exposed to new situations that require creative solutions. Letting go of old patterns and habits can further promote innovative problem-solving.

For example, someone who takes up a new hobby, such

as learning a musical instrument, may encounter challenging pieces or techniques that require creative problem-solving skills. They may need to experiment with different approaches, seek out new resources, and even collaborate with others to find solutions. In the process, they may develop new problem-solving skills that can be applied to other areas of their life.

By incorporating the practice of letting go and focusing on a greater sense of adventure, individuals can experience numerous benefits for creating space for new opportunities, promoting personal growth and self-awareness, and fostering a sense of inner peace and well-being.

Breaking Free from Old Patterns and Beliefs

We can limit ourselves and prevent personal growth and transformation when we hold onto old patterns and beliefs. For example, if we believe that we're not good enough, we may not take risks or pursue opportunities that could lead to growth and transformation. By letting go of these negative beliefs and patterns, we can break free from limiting self-perceptions and open ourselves up to new possibilities. This process can be challenging, as we often become attached to familiar patterns and beliefs, even if they're not serving us well. But by cultivating self-awareness and a willingness to let go, we can create space for personal growth and transformation. We may discover new passions, develop new skills, and become more confident in ourselves and our abilities. Ultimately, letting go of old patterns and beliefs can help us live a more fulfilling and authentic life.

Here are some key advantages of breaking free from old patterns and beliefs in terms of enhancing space for new opportunities, along with the associated benefits of letting go:

Increased self-awareness: Breaking free from old patterns and beliefs can lead to increased self-awareness as individuals become more conscious of their thoughts and behaviors. Letting go of attachment to old ways of thinking and embracing curiosity and exploration can promote greater self-awareness and personal growth.

For example, a person may have a habit of always saying "yes" to requests from others, even if they are overcommitting themselves and causing stress. By letting go of this pattern and exploring the reasons behind it, such as a fear of disappointing others or a desire to be liked, the individual may become more self-aware of their own needs and boundaries. This increased self-awareness can lead to better decision-making, improved relationships, and a greater sense of fulfillment and well-being.

Enhanced problem-solving: Breaking free from old patterns and beliefs can also contribute to enhanced problem-solving, as individuals are more open to new ideas and perspectives. Letting go of old patterns and habits can further promote innovative problem-solving.

A software developer has been working on the same project for years and has always used the same approach to solve problems that arise. However, the project has reached a critical phase where new and complex problems need to be solved. The developer realizes that the old approach is no longer effective and decides to break free from the old patterns and beliefs. They start exploring new problem-solving techniques and tools, attend workshops and conferences, and collaborate with experts in the field. As a result, the developer gains new insights and finds innovative solutions to the challenges faced in the project, leading to better outcomes and increased efficiency.

Greater adaptability: Breaking free from old patterns and beliefs can also contribute to greater adaptability, as individuals learn to be more flexible and responsive to changing circumstances. Letting go of rigidity and embracing flexibility and resilience can promote greater adaptability and openness to new experiences.

For example, imagine a person who has always been very strict about their daily routine and has a hard time deviating from it. They may find it difficult to adjust to changes in their schedule or unexpected events. However, if they begin to let go of their attachment to their routine and embrace the idea of flexibility, they may become more adaptable and better able to handle new situations. They may be more willing to try new things and take risks, which can lead to greater personal growth and fulfillment.

Improved decision-making: Breaking free from old patterns and beliefs can lead to improved decision-making, as individuals are more willing to consider new options and perspectives. Letting go of attachment to old ways of thinking and embracing a growth mindset can promote better decision-making.

An individual who has always made decisions based on what their parents or society has told them may find that they struggle with decision-making in their adult life. However, breaking free from these old patterns and beliefs makes them more open to new options and perspectives. They may start seeking advice from a variety of sources, considering multiple angles, and ultimately making choices that are more aligned with their own values and goals. This increased flexibility and openness can lead to improved decision-making in the long run.

More fulfilling and abundant life: Breaking free from old patterns and beliefs can lead to a more fulfilling and abundant life as individuals open themselves up to new experiences and possibilities. Letting go of fear and embracing courage and possibility can promote a sense of excitement and fulfillment in life.

For example, a person who has always held the belief that they are not creative may start to explore different artistic hobbies, such as painting or writing, and discover a new passion and talent that brings them a sense of fulfillment and abundance. Letting go of limiting beliefs and embracing new possibilities can open the door to a more satisfying and fulfilling life.

Greater sense of purpose: Breaking free from old patterns and beliefs can also contribute to a greater sense of purpose as individuals explore new areas of interest and passion. Letting go of limiting beliefs and embracing possibility and potential can promote a sense of inner fulfillment and purpose.

For example, someone who has always believed that they could never make a career change because it is too risky or because they don't have the right qualifications may feel unfulfilled in their current job. However, by breaking free from this limiting belief and exploring their interests and passions, they may discover a new career path that aligns with their values and gives them a greater sense of purpose. This could lead to a more fulfilling and abundant life, where they wake up every day feeling excited about their work and its impact on the world.

Improved relationships: Breaking free from old patterns and beliefs can also contribute to improved relationships, as individuals are more open to new ways of connecting and communicating. Letting go of old patterns of communication and embracing new ways of expression can promote deeper and more fulfilling relationships.

For example, let's say someone has always struggled to express their emotions in their relationships. They may have grown up in a family where emotions were not discussed openly, or they may have had negative experiences in the past where they were rejected or criticized for expressing their feelings. If they can recognize this pattern and actively work on breaking free from it, they may be more open and honest with their partner, which can lead to deeper and more fulfilling communication and connection. They may also be more receptive to their partner's emotions and be better equipped to support them in a way that strengthens their relationship.

Enhanced creativity: Breaking free from old patterns and beliefs can contribute to enhanced creativity, as individuals are more willing to explore new ideas and perspectives. Letting go of old patterns of thinking and embracing a sense of play and experimentation can promote greater creativity and innovation.

For example, an artist who has been creating in the same style or using the same techniques for years may feel like they've hit a creative wall. By breaking free from their old patterns and beliefs about what art should look like, they may experiment with new mediums or styles, leading to a burst of creativity and innovation. They may find new inspiration in nature or in the work of other artists, which they can incorporate into their own work, resulting in a more diverse and dynamic body of work.

Increased confidence: Breaking free from old patterns and beliefs can also contribute to increased confidence, as individuals learn to trust their own judgment and make choices that support their well-being. Letting go of self-doubt and embracing self-acceptance and self-love can support continued confidence and self-assurance.

For example, let's say someone has struggled with low self-esteem for years due to negative messages they received in childhood. Breaking free from the limiting belief that they are not good enough and embracing a growth mindset can lead them to start taking actions that support their own well-being and positive self-image, such as engaging in self-care activities and setting healthy boundaries. As they see the positive results of their actions and practice self-love and self-acceptance, their confidence can grow, and they may feel more empowered to make choices that align with their values and goals.

By incorporating the practice of letting go and breaking free from old patterns and beliefs, individuals can experience numerous benefits for creating space for new opportunities, promoting personal growth and self-awareness, and fostering a sense of inner peace and well-being.

Overall, letting go can help us create more space for the things that truly matter in our lives, whether that be new experiences, personal growth, or greater fulfillment.

CHAPTER 7 –
IMPROVED PHYSICAL
HEALTH

Letting go isn't just important for our mental and emotional well-being and can also significantly impact our physical health. When we hold onto negative emotions, stress, and tension, it can manifest in our bodies in a variety of ways. However, learning how to let go can improve our physical health and overall well-being.

Reduced Pain

Letting go can have a significant impact on reducing physical pain. When we hold onto negative emotions and stress, it can manifest in physical ways, such as chronic headaches, back pain, and joint pain. By letting go and releasing these negative emotions, we can reduce the impact they have on our physical health.

Studies have shown that stress and negative emotions can contribute to chronic pain by increasing inflammation in the body. When we let go, we can reduce this inflammation and, in turn, reduce pain. Additionally, letting go can help us develop better coping mechanisms for dealing with pain and stress, leading to greater control over our physical health.

Letting go can also improve our physical function by reducing tension in the body. Holding onto stress and negative emotions can cause our muscles to tense up, leading to stiffness and decreased mobility. Letting go can release this tension and improve our physical function and range of motion.

Here are some key advantages of reduced pain in terms of improving physical health, along with the associated benefits of letting go:

Improved mobility: Reduced pain can lead to improved mobility, as individuals are better able to move without discomfort or limitations. Letting go of attachment to old patterns of movement and embracing new ways of moving can promote continued mobility and flexibility.

For example, a person who has been experiencing chronic back pain may have avoided certain movements or activities out of fear of exacerbating their pain. However, with reduced pain through treatment or therapy, they may feel more comfortable exploring new movements and activities that they previously avoided. This can lead to improved mobility, as they are now able to move more freely and with less pain. By letting go of their attachment to old patterns of movement and embracing new ways of moving, such as engaging in regular exercise or trying new forms of physical activity, they can promote continued mobility and flexibility.

Enhanced physical function: Reduced pain can also contribute to enhanced physical function, as individuals can perform daily activities and tasks better. Letting go of attachment to old limitations and embracing new possibilities can promote continued physical function and independence.

Increased energy: Reduced pain can lead to increased energy, as individuals are no longer expending energy coping with discomfort or managing pain. Letting go of attachment to old patterns of energy and embracing new ways of vitality and health can promote greater energy and vitality.

Improved sleep: Reduced pain can also contribute to improved sleep, as individuals are better able to rest without discomfort or interruption. Letting go of attachment to old patterns of sleep and embracing new ways of relaxation and rest can promote better sleep hygiene and improved overall sleep quality.

Enhanced mental health: Reduced pain can have positive effects on mental health, as individuals are better able to focus on activities and experiences that bring them joy and fulfillment. Letting go of attachment to old pain patterns and embracing new coping and healing methods can promote greater mental resilience and positivity.

Improved overall health: Reduced pain can contribute to improved overall health, as individuals are better able to engage in healthy activities and pursue wellness goals. Letting go of attachment to old patterns of health and embracing new ways of well-being and vitality can promote continued improvement in overall health.

By incorporating the practice of letting go and focusing on reduced pain, individuals can experience numerous benefits for improving physical health, promoting personal growth and self-awareness, and fostering a sense of inner peace and well-being.

Improved Sleep

When we're holding onto negative emotions, it can create a constant undercurrent of stress and anxiety. This can make it difficult to fall asleep, stay asleep, or get restful sleep. On the other hand, letting go of these emotions can help us release that tension and improve our sleep. When we get enough restful sleep, our bodies are better able to repair and regenerate, which is essential for our physical health. Improved sleep can also lead to other benefits, such as more energy, improved mood, and better cognitive function. So, letting go of negative emotions can profoundly impact our physical health and well-being.

Here are some key advantages of improved sleep, in terms of improving physical health, along with the associated benefits of letting go:

Increased immune function: Improved sleep can lead to increased immune function, as the body is better able to produce and distribute immune cells. Letting go of attachment to stress and worry and embracing new ways of relaxation and rest can promote a stronger immune system.

Improved physical performance: Improved sleep can also contribute to improved physical performance, as individuals are better able to perform physical activities and exercises. Letting go of attachment to old patterns of fatigue and embracing new ways of vitality and energy can promote improved physical performance.

Reduced inflammation: Improved sleep can lead to reduced inflammation, as the body is better able to regulate its inflammatory response. Letting go of attachment to stress and worry and embracing new ways of relaxation and rest can promote reduced inflammation and improved overall health.

Improved cardiovascular health: Improved sleep can also contribute to improved cardiovascular health, as the body is better able to regulate blood pressure and heart rate. Letting go of attachment to old patterns of stress and anxiety and embracing new ways of relaxation and rest can promote improved cardiovascular health and reduced risk of heart disease.

Reduced risk of obesity: Improved sleep can lead to a reduced risk of obesity, as individuals are less likely to engage in late-night snacking or overeating due to fatigue or stress. Letting go of attachment to old patterns of emotional eating and embracing new ways of self-care and nourishment can promote improved eating habits and reduce the risk of obesity.

Improved hormonal balance: Improved sleep can also contribute to improved hormonal balance, as the body is better able to regulate the production and distribution of hormones. Letting go of attachment to old patterns of stress and worry and embracing new ways of relaxation and rest can promote improved hormonal balance and overall health.

Enhanced physical recovery: Improved sleep can also contribute to enhanced physical recovery, as the body is better able to repair and regenerate damaged tissues. Letting go of attachment to old patterns of stress and anxiety and embracing new ways of rest and recovery can promote improved physical healing and overall well-being.

By incorporating the practice of letting go and focusing on improved sleep, individuals can experience numerous benefits for improving physical health, promoting personal growth and self-awareness, and fostering a sense of inner peace and well-being.

Lowered Blood Pressure

Holding onto negative emotions can create a chronic state of stress in our bodies, which can increase our blood pressure. Over time, this can contribute to heart disease, stroke, and other health issues. Letting go of stress and negative emotions can help lower our blood pressure and improve our overall cardiovascular health. In fact, studies have shown that practicing stress reduction techniques, such as meditation and deep breathing, can help lower blood pressure and reduce the risk of heart disease. So, by learning to let go, we can improve our mental and emotional health and physical health.

Here are some key advantages of lowered blood pressure in terms of improving physical health, along with the associated benefits of letting go:

Reduced risk of heart disease: Lowered blood pressure can lead to a reduced risk of heart disease, as high blood pressure is a major risk factor for heart disease. Letting go of attachment to stress and worry and embracing new relaxation and stress management methods can promote a healthier heart and reduce the risk of heart disease.

Improved kidney function: Lowered blood pressure can also contribute to improved kidney function, as high blood pressure can cause damage to the kidneys over time. Letting go of attachment to old stress and anxiety patterns and embracing new relaxation and self-care can promote healthier kidneys and overall kidney function.

Reduced risk of stroke: Lowered blood pressure can lead to a reduced risk of stroke, as high blood pressure is a major risk factor for stroke. Letting go of attachment to old patterns of stress and worry and embracing new relaxation and stress management methods can promote a healthier brain and reduce the risk of stroke.

Improved vision: Lowered blood pressure can also

contribute to improved vision, as high blood pressure can cause damage to the blood vessels in the eyes. Letting go of attachment to old stress and anxiety patterns and embracing new relaxation and self-care methods can promote healthier eyes and improved vision.

Reduced risk of cognitive decline: Lowered blood pressure can lead to a reduced risk of cognitive decline, as high blood pressure has been linked to cognitive impairment and dementia. Letting go of attachment to old patterns of stress and worry and embracing new relaxation and stress management methods can promote a healthier brain and reduce the risk of cognitive decline.

Enhanced overall physical health: Lowered blood pressure can contribute to enhanced overall physical health, as the body is better able to regulate blood flow and maintain optimal organ function. Letting go of attachment to old stress and anxiety patterns and embracing new relaxation and self-care can promote improved physical health and well-being.

By incorporating the practice of letting go and focusing on lowered blood pressure, individuals can experience numerous benefits for improving physical health, promoting personal growth and self-awareness, and fostering a sense of inner peace and well-being.

Strengthened Immune System

When we experience chronic stress and negative emotions can take a toll on our physical health and weaken our immune system. This can leave us vulnerable to illnesses and diseases. By letting go of stress and negative emotions, we can actually strengthen our immune system and improve our overall health. When we're not constantly under stress, our body can focus on healing and repairing itself, and our immune system can function more efficiently. This means we're less likely to get sick and more able to recover quickly if we do. So, by learning to let go, we can improve our mental and emotional health, physical health, and well-being.

Here are some key advantages of a strengthened immune system in terms of improving physical health, along with the associated benefits of letting go:

Reduced risk of infections: A strengthened immune system can lead to a reduced risk of infections, as the body is better able to defend itself against harmful bacteria and viruses. Letting go of attachment to old stress and anxiety patterns and embracing new relaxation and self-care can promote a strengthened immune system and reduce the risk of infections.

Improved recovery from illness: A strengthened immune system can also contribute to improved recovery from illness, as the body is better able to fight off infection and heal itself. Letting go of attachment to old patterns of negative thinking and embracing new ways of self-care and positivity can promote improved immune function and quicker recovery from illness.

Reduced risk of chronic diseases: A strengthened immune system can lead to a reduced risk of chronic diseases, such as heart disease, cancer, and diabetes. Letting go of attachment to old stress and anxiety patterns and embracing new relaxation and stress management methods can promote a strengthened immune system and reduce the risk of chronic diseases.

Improved overall physical health: A strengthened immune system can contribute to improved overall physical health, as the body is better able to maintain optimal organ function and resist illness. Letting go of attachment to old stress and anxiety patterns and embracing new self-care and healthy lifestyle habits can promote improved physical health and well-being.

Improved mental health: A strengthened immune system can also contribute to improved mental health, as individuals are better able to maintain optimal brain function and resist illnesses such as depression and anxiety. Letting go of attachment to old negative thinking patterns and embracing new ways of self-care and positivity can promote improved immune function and mental health.

By incorporating the practice of letting go and focusing on a strengthened immune system, individuals can experience numerous benefits for improving physical health, promoting personal growth and self-awareness, and fostering a sense of inner peace and well-being.

Reduced Inflammation

Chronic stress and negative emotions can trigger an inflammatory response in the body, which can lead to a range of health problems, from skin issues to heart disease. Inflammation can even exacerbate pre-existing conditions such as arthritis and asthma. Letting go of stress and negative emotions can help reduce inflammation in the body and promote overall physical health. When we're not holding onto negative emotions, we're less likely to experience stress and anxiety, which in turn can lower inflammation levels in the body. This can lead to improved overall physical health and a reduced risk of chronic diseases.

Here are some key advantages of reduced inflammation in terms of improving physical health, along with the associated benefits of letting go:

Reduced risk of chronic diseases: Reduced inflammation can lead to a reduced risk of chronic diseases, such as heart disease, diabetes, and cancer, as chronic inflammation has been linked to the development of these diseases. Letting go of attachment to stress and worry and embracing new relaxation and stress management methods can promote reduced inflammation and improved overall health.

Improved joint health: Reduced inflammation can also contribute to improved joint health, as inflammation can cause damage to joint tissue and lead to conditions such as arthritis. Letting go of attachment to old patterns of stress and anxiety and embracing new ways of self-care and movement can promote healthier joints and improved overall mobility.

Improved digestive health: Reduced inflammation can lead to improved digestive health, as chronic inflammation can contribute to digestive disorders such as irritable bowel syndrome (IBS) and inflammatory bowel disease (IBD). Letting go of attachment to old patterns of stress and anxiety and embracing new ways of self-care and healthy eating can promote improved digestive function and overall health.

Improved skin health: Reduced inflammation can also contribute to improved skin health, as chronic inflammation can contribute to skin conditions such as acne, psoriasis, and eczema. Letting go of attachment to old patterns of stress and anxiety and embracing new ways of self-care and healthy lifestyle habits can promote clearer, healthier skin.

Enhanced overall physical health: Reduced inflammation can contribute to enhanced overall physical health, as the body is better able to regulate inflammation and maintain optimal organ function. Letting go of attachment to old stress and anxiety patterns and embracing new relaxation and self-care can promote improved physical health and well-being.

By incorporating the practice of letting go and focusing on reduced inflammation, individuals can experience numerous benefits for improving physical health, promoting personal growth and self-awareness, and fostering a sense of inner peace and well-being.

Increased Energy

Letting go of negative emotions and stress can significantly impact our energy levels. When we're holding onto something, it can feel like a weight on our shoulders, draining our energy and motivation. But when we let go, we release that tension and free up space for new energy and vitality.

Letting go can help us feel lighter, both physically and mentally. We're no longer carrying the burden of negative emotions or stress, and we're able to approach life with renewed energy and enthusiasm. This can help us tackle our daily tasks with greater ease and efficiency and even take on new challenges that we may have previously felt too overwhelmed to attempt.

In addition, letting go can help us get better quality sleep, which can also contribute to increased energy levels. When we're not holding onto negative emotions or stress, we're able to relax more fully and fall asleep more easily. This can lead to more restful, rejuvenating sleep, which can leave us feeling more refreshed and energized in the morning.

Overall, letting go can be a powerful tool for increasing our energy levels and improving our overall physical health. By releasing negative emotions and stress, we can tap into a new source of energy and vitality, allowing us to approach life with renewed enthusiasm and vigor.

Here are some key advantages of increased energy in terms of improving physical health, along with the associated benefits of letting go:

Improved physical performance: Increased energy can lead to improved physical performance, as individuals are better able to perform physical activities and exercises. Letting go of attachment to old patterns of fatigue and embracing new ways of vitality and energy can promote improved physical performance and overall fitness.

Enhanced overall physical health: Increased energy can

contribute to enhanced overall physical health, as individuals are better able to engage in healthy lifestyle habits such as regular exercise, healthy eating, and stress management. Letting go of attachment to old stress and anxiety patterns and embracing new relaxation and self-care can promote improved physical health and well-being.

Improved cardiovascular health: Increased energy can also contribute to improved cardiovascular health, as individuals are better able to engage in physical activities that promote heart health. Letting go of attachment to old stress and anxiety patterns and embracing new relaxation and stress management methods can promote improved cardiovascular health and reduced risk of heart disease.

Reduced risk of obesity: Increased energy can lead to a reduced risk of obesity, as individuals are more likely to engage in physical activities and healthy eating habits that support weight management. Letting go of attachment to old patterns of emotional eating and embracing new ways of self-care and nourishment can promote improved eating habits and reduce the risk of obesity.

Improved sleep: Increased energy can also contribute to improved sleep, as individuals are better able to maintain healthy sleep patterns and get the rest they need. Letting go of attachment to old stress and anxiety patterns and embracing new relaxation and stress management methods can promote improved sleep and overall health.

By incorporating the practice of letting go and focusing on increased energy, individuals can experience numerous benefits for improving physical health, promoting personal growth and self-awareness, and fostering a sense of inner peace and well-being.

Overall, learning how to let go can profoundly impact our lives in the short and long term. It can help us reduce stress and anxiety, improve our relationships, create space for new opportunities, and support our personal growth and transformation. By embracing the art of letting go, we can live more fully and authentically and create the lives we truly desire.

CHAPTER 8 - OBSTACLES TO LETTING GO

Obstacles to letting go can vary depending on the person and the situation. However, some common obstacles include fear, attachment, and a lack of awareness or understanding of the benefits of letting go.

Fear is a powerful emotion that can hold us back from letting go of something that is no longer serving us. We may fear the unknown or fear what will happen if we let go. For example, we may fear losing a job, a relationship, or a sense of identity. This fear can be paralyzing and make it difficult to take the necessary steps to let go.

Attachment is another obstacle to letting go. We may be attached to a person, place, or thing and feel like we cannot let go without losing a part of ourselves. We may have sentimental attachments or feel like we have invested too much time and effort to let go. This attachment can create a sense of loss and make it difficult to move forward.

A lack of awareness or understanding of the benefits of letting go can also be an obstacle. We may not realize that holding onto something is causing us stress or hindering our personal growth. We may not understand that letting go can create space for new opportunities or lead to greater inner peace and contentment.

Overall, it's important to recognize and address these obstacles to successfully let go and move forward in a positive and meaningful way.

While letting go can be transformative, it's not always easy. There are several common obstacles that can make it difficult to let go of something. Below are a few of them to discuss.

Fear of the Unknown

One of the biggest obstacles to letting go is fear of the unknown. When we're holding onto something, it's often because it feels safe and familiar. Letting go can mean stepping into the unknown, which can be scary and uncomfortable. Here are a few specific ways that fear of the unknown can be an obstacle to letting go:

Fear of change: Fear of change is a common obstacle to letting go. Feeling apprehensive about what might happen when we let go of something familiar and step into the unknown is natural. We may worry that we'll lose our sense of security or stability or that we'll regret our decision later. These fears can be so strong that they keep us stuck in unhealthy situations, relationships, or patterns, even if we know deep down that they're not serving us. It takes courage and a willingness to embrace the unknown to overcome this obstacle and move forward in a positive direction.

Let's say you have lived in the same city and have always been surrounded by the same community and familiar surroundings. However, deep down, you have always felt a strong desire to explore and travel the world. You dream of experiencing new cultures and ways of life, but the fear of leaving behind everything you have known and loved for so long keeps holding you back.

You might fear the uncertainty of traveling, being alone in unfamiliar surroundings, or missing out on important events or moments back home. These fears can prevent you from acting and pursuing your dreams.

However, if you can find the courage to let go of these fears and take a leap of faith, you may discover new experiences, opportunities, and perspectives that you never thought possible. You may discover a new sense of fulfillment and purpose in life that you would have never found if you had held onto your fears and stayed in your comfort zone.

Fear of loss: Fear of loss can be a major obstacle to letting go. It's natural to feel attached to familiar and comfortable things, even if they may not be serving us well. Letting go can mean giving up something we value, and that can be scary. We may worry that we'll never find something as good or that we'll be worse off without it. This fear can hold us back from making the necessary changes to move forward and grow. It's important to acknowledge and accept our feelings of loss but also to remember that letting go can create space for new opportunities and experiences in our lives. Focusing on what we stand to gain by letting go rather than just what we're giving up can be helpful.

For example, Samantha had been in a toxic relationship with her partner for several years. Although she knew deep down that it wasn't healthy for her, she was afraid to let go because she feared losing the love and companionship that she had grown accustomed to. Even though her partner often treated her poorly and made her feel small, Samantha couldn't imagine life without them. The thought of being alone and starting over from scratch was terrifying to her. Despite her unhappiness, she continued to hold onto the relationship because the fear of losing what she had outweighed the potential benefits of letting go and moving on to something better.

Fear of the future: Fear of the future is a common obstacle to letting go. We often hold onto things because they provide a sense of security and familiarity. But letting go means stepping out of our comfort zones and into the unknown, which can be scary. We may fear that we won't be able to handle what comes next or that we'll make the wrong decisions. This fear can hold us back from making the necessary changes for growth and transformation. It's important to remember that the future is never certain and that taking risks and embracing uncertainty can lead to new opportunities and experiences. By letting go of our fear of the future, we can create space for growth and positive change in our lives.

Imagine someone who has been in a stable job for many years but is feeling unfulfilled and wants to pursue a new career path. They may feel apprehensive about letting go of their current job because they are unsure of what the future holds. They may worry about financial instability or not being successful in their new career. This fear of the unknown future can be a major obstacle in letting go of their current job and pursuing their dreams.

Fear of losing control: Fear of losing control can also be a common obstacle to letting go. We may feel like holding onto something gives us a sense of control over our lives, and letting go can feel like giving that up. It can be scary to think about what might happen if we don't have that control anymore. We may also worry about what others will think of us if we let go of control or whether we'll be able to handle the consequences of not being in control. This fear can be particularly strong for those who struggle with anxiety or have experienced trauma in their lives.

For example, John is a manager at a company and has a very controlling personality. He likes to micromanage his team and ensure that everything is done exactly as he wants it to be. However, due to some unforeseen circumstances, John had to take a few weeks off from work, leaving his team in charge of a big project. During his absence, John felt anxious and stressed out, constantly checking in on his team and feeling like he was losing control of the situation. When he returned to work, he found that his team had completed the project successfully, but he couldn't help feeling like he had missed out on the process and that things could have gone wrong if he hadn't been there to control every detail. This fear of losing control can prevent John from delegating tasks and trusting his team in the future, limiting his growth as a leader and hindering his team's success.

Fear of failure: Fear of failure is a common obstacle

when it comes to letting go. We may hold onto things, even if they're not serving us well, because we're afraid of what might happen if we let them go. We may worry that we'll fail in our future endeavors or that we won't be able to cope without what we're holding onto. This fear can keep us stuck in a negative cycle, preventing us from moving forward and experiencing new opportunities. It's important to remember that failure is a natural part of the learning process and can lead to growth and eventual success. By letting go of the fear of failure, we can open ourselves up to new possibilities and experiences.

Let's say, for example, someone is considering starting their own business. They have a great idea and the skills to make it happen but are hesitant to take the leap because they fear failure. They worry that if the business doesn't succeed, it will be seen as a failure themselves. They may also be worried about the financial risks and their impact on their personal life. As a result, they may hold themselves back from pursuing their dream, even though it's something they truly want to do. This fear of failure can prevent them from taking risks and trying new things, ultimately holding them back from personal growth and success.

Fear of success: Fear of success is another common obstacle to letting go. Sometimes we hold onto negative beliefs or patterns because we fear what might happen if we succeed. This fear can stem from a variety of sources, such as a fear of change or a fear of the unknown.

For example, someone might hold onto a dead-end job or an unfulfilling relationship because they're afraid of the responsibility and pressure that come with success. Or they might believe that they don't deserve success, and so they sabotage themselves to avoid the possibility of achieving their goals.

But the truth is that success can bring about many positive changes in our lives. It can bring a sense of accomplishment, financial stability, and personal growth. By letting go of our fears and allowing ourselves to succeed, we can experience these benefits and more.

It's important to recognize and acknowledge our fears of success and work through them to let go of any limiting beliefs or patterns. This might involve seeking support from a therapist or coach, practicing self-compassion, and setting realistic goals for us. By doing so, we can overcome this obstacle and move forward toward a more fulfilling and successful life.

Attachment to the Past,
Present, or Future

Many of us have experienced a strong attachment to the past at some point in our lives. We may find ourselves constantly dwelling on past mistakes, holding onto past hurts or regrets, or feeling stuck in old habits and routines. This attachment to the past can be a major obstacle to letting go and moving forward in a positive direction. In the following sections, we'll explore some of the common ways that attachment to the past can hold us back and provide some tips on how to let go and embrace the future.

Another potential attachment is with the present. This may not seem too obvious, but trying to maintain your current situation may be undesirable. It is much less common than holding on to your past but can be an issue. Usually, attachment to the present masks your attachment to the past. That said, true attachment to the present typically comes when you have broken the chains of the past. You are attempting to live in the moment – the here and now. This creates a situation where you are now attached to the detachment. Very confusing indeed – something you generally don't have to worry about until you get there. The final step is detaching from detachment – a whole other conversation for the more advanced individuals on their journey of letting go.

As for the future, this too can also become a roadblock to letting go. In some cases, you hold on to ideas and thoughts about the future, hoping for a better life. Embracing the future can certainly be a good thing, but we must be careful not to dwell on it too much. Being attached to the future can be just as bad as being attached to the past. You must also let go of the future to some extent. Rather, you are letting go of preordained notions of what your future must look like. Having goals and expectations for the future provides great value in life. But when you become attached to them and not willing to be flexible, you can lose sight of your true goals, which should be more aligned with living with joy and happiness in the present moment.

Nostalgia: Nostalgia can be a powerful emotion that can keep us attached to the past. It's natural to want to hold onto memories of happy times or special moments, but sometimes we can get stuck in the past and not want to move forward. We might hold onto old items or keep revisiting certain places or events because they remind us of a time in our lives that we enjoyed. However, it's important to recognize that we can't go back in time and relive those moments and that holding onto them too tightly can prevent us from creating new experiences and memories. It can be difficult to let go of something that we associate with happy memories, but it's important to remember that we can still cherish those memories without clinging to physical objects or past experiences.

Let's say someone has a tattered and worn-out shirt that they've had since they were teenagers. Although it's no longer wearable, they can't bring themselves to throw it away because it reminds them of happy memories from their youth. They may hold onto the shirt to feel connected to that time in their life and the associated memories, even though it no longer serves a practical purpose. This attachment to the past can make it difficult for them to let go of the shirt and move on.

Sentimentality: Sentimentality is a common obstacle to letting go. We may have a strong emotional attachment to something because it represents a special memory or connection to someone we love. For example, maybe we have a favorite sweater that was given to us by our grandmother, and even though it no longer fits or is in poor condition, we can't bear to part with it because it reminds us of her. This sentimental attachment can make it difficult to let go of the sweater, even if it's no longer serving us in any practical way. The fear of losing that sentimental value can hold us back from making the decision to let go.

Let's say that you have a necklace that was given to you by your grandmother before she passed away. You never wear the necklace, but you keep it in a jewelry box because it holds sentimental value to you. However, you're moving to a new home and trying to declutter your belongings. You know that you don't have any use for the necklace and it's just taking up space, but you're hesitant to let it go because it reminds you of your grandmother and the memories you shared with her.

Comfort: Sometimes, we hold onto things because they provide us with a sense of comfort and security. For example, we may have a favorite pair of old, worn-out shoes that we refuse to throw away because they feel familiar and comfortable. Similarly, we may hold onto an unfulfilling job or relationship because it's what we know and feels safer than the unknown. However, this attachment to comfort can prevent us from pursuing new experiences and opportunities that could bring greater fulfillment and happiness. It's important to recognize when we're holding onto something simply because it's comfortable and to be open to stepping out of our comfort zone for the sake of personal growth and transformation.

Let's say you have a job that you've been doing for several years, and even though it's not fulfilling and doesn't align with your passions and interests, you feel comfortable and secure in it. You know the routine, you're familiar with the people and the environment, and you don't want to risk losing that sense of comfort and security by letting go of the job and pursuing something new and unknown. So, you continue to hold onto the job, even though it's not bringing you true happiness or fulfillment.

Regret: Regret is another obstacle to letting go. We may be holding onto something because we regret a decision we made in the past and feel like we need to hold onto it as a reminder of that regret. This can be particularly true when it comes to relationships or opportunities that we passed up. We might feel like if we let go of that thing, we're admitting that we made a mistake and are incapable of making the right decision in the future. This fear of making the same mistake again can hold us back from letting go and moving forward.

An example of attachment to the past in a parent-child relationship could be a parent who is holding onto their child's childhood, even as the child grows into adulthood. The parent may still treat the child as if they are young and dependent and struggle to let go of the role of protector and caregiver. This can cause tension and strain in the relationship as the child seeks independence and the freedom to make their own choices. The parent may feel a sense of loss and regret as they realize that their child is no longer a child and struggle to adjust to the new dynamic of the relationship.

Trauma: Trauma can be a significant obstacle to letting go of past experiences or emotions. Traumatic events can have a lasting impact on our lives and may cause us to feel stuck in the past. The fear, pain, and helplessness that often accompany trauma can make it difficult to move on and let go. It can also trigger anxiety, depression, and other mental health issues that can further impede our ability to let go.

For example, a person who has experienced a traumatic event like a car accident may find it challenging to get behind the wheel of a car again, even if it's been years since the incident. The fear and anxiety associated with the traumatic event may continue to linger, causing them to avoid driving altogether. In this case, letting go of the trauma and associated emotions may require professional help, such as therapy or counseling. With support, it is possible to work through trauma and let go of the hold it has on our lives.

Identification: Identification is an obstacle that can make it difficult to let go of something because we have attached our identity to it. This could be a job title, a role we play in our family or community, or a belief or ideology that we strongly identify with. When we attach our identity to something, we may feel like letting go of it would mean losing a part of ourselves.

For example, someone who has identified as a workaholic may find it difficult to let go of their busy schedule and take a break, even if it's causing burnout and stress. They may feel like they are losing a part of their identity if they're not working constantly. Similarly, someone who strongly identifies with a particular political party may have a hard time letting go of their beliefs, even when presented with new information or perspectives that challenge their views.

Identification can make it difficult to let go because we fear losing a part of ourselves. However, it's important to remember that our identity is not fixed, and we can adapt and evolve over time. Letting go of attachments that no longer serve us can help us discover new aspects of ourselves and grow in unexpected ways.

External pressures or expectations: External pressures or expectations refer to societal or cultural expectations, family values, or pressure from peers or authority figures that may impact our ability to let go. We may feel obligated to hold onto something because it's what's expected of us or because we fear judgment or rejection if we don't.

For example, a person may have a family business that they are expected to take over, even if they don't have a passion for it or it doesn't align with their personal goals. The pressure from family members and the fear of disappointing them may make it difficult for them to let go of the business and pursue their own path.

Another example could be a person who has been raised in a particular cultural or religious tradition and feels pressure to continue to adhere to its customs and beliefs, even if they no longer resonate with them. The fear of being ostracized or judged by their community can make it challenging for them to let go and explore new perspectives or ways of living.

These external pressures or expectations can be

significant obstacles in letting go and require much courage and introspection to overcome. It's important to remember that, ultimately, our lives belong to us, and we have the right to make choices that align with our values and aspirations, even if it means letting go of something deeply ingrained in our social or cultural identity.

The Future: Attachment to the future is a common experience that can impact our ability to enjoy the present moment and lead to stress and anxiety. While planning and preparing for the future is natural, excessive attachment to specific outcomes or expectations can be problematic. This attachment can manifest in a variety of ways, including worrying about future outcomes, setting rigid expectations, avoiding present experiences, and holding onto negative emotions related to past experiences. It's important to strike a balance between planning for the future and living in the present, and letting go of excessive attachment to specific outcomes or expectations can lead to greater happiness and fulfillment in life.

Here are some examples of attachment to the future:

Constantly worrying about future outcomes: This may involve obsessing over potential negative consequences and feeling anxious about what may happen in the future.

Setting rigid expectations for the future: This may involve placing high pressure on oneself to achieve specific goals and feeling upset or disappointed if these expectations are not met.

Avoiding present experiences to focus on the future: This may involve putting off enjoying present experiences, such as spending time with loved ones or pursuing hobbies, to focus solely on future goals.

Holding onto grudges or negative emotions related to past experiences that impact future outcomes: This may involve holding onto anger or resentment towards someone, which can impact future relationships and opportunities.

Feeling like the future is the only source of happiness: This may involve placing all happiness and fulfillment in future events or accomplishments, which can lead to feelings of disappointment and unhappiness in the present.

Overall, attachment to the future can be problematic when it prevents individuals from fully enjoying the present moment and engaging in healthy relationships and experiences. It's important to maintain a balance between planning for the future and enjoying the present and to let go of excessive attachment to specific outcomes or expectations.

Lack of Self-Awareness

A lack of self-awareness can make it difficult to recognize the need to let go of something in the first place. For example, let's say someone has a pattern of constantly seeking validation from others and has a hard time feeling confident in their own abilities. They may not be aware that their need for validation is holding them back and preventing them from taking risks or pursuing their goals. Without self-awareness, they may continue to seek validation from others and not realize that it's preventing them from growing and achieving their full potential.

In this scenario, developing self-awareness through introspection, therapy, or other practices can help them recognize the need to let go of the need for constant validation and shift their focus toward building their self-confidence and pursuing their goals.

Here are a few specific ways that a lack of self-awareness can be an obstacle to letting go:

Difficulty recognizing negative patterns: Difficulty recognizing negative patterns can be a major obstacle to letting go. When we're not self-aware, we may not even realize that we're engaging in negative behavior or thought patterns. For example, we might have a habit of always blaming others for our problems, or we might be overly critical of ourselves. These negative patterns can hold us back and prevent us from making positive changes in our lives.

Without self-awareness, it can be difficult to recognize these patterns and take steps to address them. We might continue to blame others or beat ourselves up without realizing that these behaviors are not serving us. To let go of these negative patterns, we need first to become aware of them and acknowledge that they exist. Only then can we begin to work on changing them and letting go of the negative thoughts and behaviors that are holding us back.

Let's say someone grew up in a household where their parents constantly criticized them. As a result, they developed a negative pattern of thinking where they are overly self-critical and never feel good enough. They may not even realize that this is a negative pattern because it's been with them for so long. As an adult, they may struggle in their relationships because they have a hard time believing that anyone could truly love and accept them. In this case, the person's lack of self-awareness about their negative thinking pattern is an obstacle in letting go of their negative self-perceptions and moving towards healthier relationships.

Lack of understanding of personal values: When we lack self-awareness, we may not fully understand our personal values, what's important to us, and what we truly want in life. This can make it difficult to let go of things that are not aligned with our values and goals or to recognize when we're holding onto something that is not serving us.

For example, if someone values honesty and transparency in their relationships but they find themselves holding onto a friendship with someone who has repeatedly lied to them, they may struggle to let go of that friendship because they haven't fully recognized the importance of honesty in their life. Without this understanding of their values, they may continue to hold onto the friendship even though it is causing them pain and harm.

On the other hand, if someone clearly understands their values, they may be more likely to recognize when a situation or relationship is not aligned with those values and be more willing to let go to stay true to themselves.

Inability to recognize limiting beliefs: Another obstacle to letting go is the inability to recognize limiting beliefs. These are the beliefs that we hold about ourselves or the world that hold us back from achieving our goals and living our best lives.

For example, if we believe we're not smart enough to pursue a certain career, we may hold ourselves back from trying. It can be challenging to let go of these beliefs because they often become deeply ingrained in our minds over time.

Without self-awareness, it can be difficult to recognize these limiting beliefs and their impact on our lives. We may not even realize that we're holding ourselves back. Only when we become more self-aware and begin to question our beliefs can we start to identify and challenge these limiting beliefs. By doing so, we can let go of the beliefs that are holding us back and open ourselves up to new opportunities for growth and transformation.

Resistance to change: Resistance to change is a common obstacle in letting go. Change can be scary and uncertain, and it's natural to want to cling to what's familiar and comfortable. However, resisting change can prevent us from growing and transforming and can keep us stuck in unhealthy patterns and situations.

One reason we may resist change is fear of the unknown. We may be uncertain about what the future holds and feel more comfortable staying in our current situation, even if it's not ideal. Another reason is fear of failure. We may worry that if we try something new or let go of something old, we'll fail or make things worse.

Another reason we may resist change is a sense of loss. We may be attached to certain people, habits, or beliefs, and letting go of them can feel like we're losing a part of ourselves. This can be especially challenging if we've been holding onto something for a long time.

Lastly, sometimes we resist change simply because it's difficult. Change requires effort, commitment, and a willingness to step outside of our comfort zone. It can be tempting to stay in familiar territory and avoid the hard work of growth and transformation.

To overcome resistance to change, it's important to cultivate self-awareness and understanding of our values and goals. We can also practice mindfulness and acceptance, acknowledging our fears and discomfort without letting them control us. Finally, seeking support from others and taking small, manageable steps toward change can help us build momentum and gain confidence.

Difficulty setting boundaries: difficulty setting boundaries can be an obstacle to letting go because it can prevent us from taking the necessary steps to prioritize our own well-being. When we struggle to set boundaries with others, we may find ourselves constantly taking on responsibilities or tasks that drain us, leaving little energy or motivation to let go of negative emotions or situations.

For example, imagine you have a friend who is always coming to you with their problems and venting about their issues but never asks how you are doing or takes the time to listen to your own struggles. You may find it difficult to set boundaries with this friend and say no to their requests for support out of fear of hurting their feelings or damaging the friendship. As a result, you may feel emotionally drained and find it hard to let go of any negative emotions you're experiencing.

In this case, setting clear boundaries with your friend and communicating your needs could help you prioritize your well-being and create space for letting go of any negative emotions or stress you're carrying.

Guilt and Shame

Guilt and shame can be powerful emotions that can hold us back from letting go. Whether it's feeling guilty about past mistakes or ashamed of who we are, these emotions can create a sense of unworthiness that makes it difficult to move on. In this section, we'll explore how guilt and shame can be obstacles to letting go and some strategies for overcoming them.

Feeling unworthy of letting go: Feeling unworthy of letting go can be a major obstacle to releasing negative emotions and patterns. This can stem from a sense of low self-esteem, self-doubt, or a belief that we don't deserve to be happy or free from suffering. It's important to recognize that everyone deserves to let go of what is holding them back and move towards a more fulfilling life.

Here are a few ways to overcome this obstacle:

Practice self-compassion: Be kind and gentle with yourself and recognize that everyone has struggles and imperfections. Treat yourself as you would a good friend.

Challenge negative self-talk: Notice when negative thoughts arise and challenge them with more positive and realistic thoughts. For example, if you find yourself thinking, "I'm not good enough," remind yourself of your strengths and accomplishments.

Seek support: Talk to a trusted friend, family member, or therapist about your feelings of unworthiness. They can provide a different perspective and offer encouragement.

By recognizing our worth and practicing self-compassion, we can overcome feelings of unworthiness and allow ourselves to let go and move forward.

Fear of judgment: Fear of judgment is another obstacle that can prevent us from letting go. We may worry about what others will think if we make a change or let go of something that's been a part of our identity. This fear can be especially strong if we feel like we're not living up to the expectations of others or if we fear being rejected or criticized.

Sometimes, we may even internalize the judgment of others and feel like we're not worthy of letting go. We may feel like we're not good enough or that we'll never be able to change. This can make it difficult to take the necessary steps to let go and move forward.

An example of fear of judgment related to sexuality could be a person who is struggling to let go of their past experiences with sexual shame and guilt. This person may have grown up in a conservative environment where sexuality was seen as taboo and sinful, and as a result, they may have internalized feelings of shame and guilt around their own sexuality.

Even though this person may now intellectually understand that there is nothing inherently wrong with expressing their sexuality healthily and consensually, they may still struggle to let go of those old beliefs and feelings of shame. This could lead to them feeling unworthy of experiencing sexual pleasure or feeling like they will be judged or rejected if they express their true desires and needs to their partner. As a result, they may hold back and struggle to let go and embrace their sexuality fully.

It's important to remember that we can't control the thoughts and opinions of others. We can only control our own actions and decisions. Letting go may require courage and vulnerability, but ultimately it's about doing what's best for ourselves and our personal growth.

We can also seek out support from those who love and accept us for who we are. Talking to a trusted friend or seeking the guidance of a therapist can help us work through our fears and gain the confidence to let go and move forward.

Fear of repeating past mistakes: Fear of repeating past mistakes is a common obstacle to letting go. We may be holding onto something because we're afraid of making the same mistakes we made in the past, or we may be afraid of making new mistakes. This fear can prevent us from taking risks or trying new things and can keep us stuck in the same patterns. We may also feel like we're not capable of making better choices, which can lead to a sense of hopelessness and a lack of motivation to change.

For example, someone who has been in an abusive relationship in the past may be afraid of letting go and moving on to a new relationship because they fear that they will repeat the same patterns and end up in another abusive situation. This fear can prevent them from trusting others and from taking the necessary steps to move on and build a healthy relationship. It may take time and effort to work through these fears and build the confidence to make different choices in the future.

Feeling responsible for others' feelings: Feeling responsible for others' feelings can be a significant obstacle to letting go. We may be holding onto something because we're worried about how it will affect someone else, even if it's not serving us. This can be especially true in close relationships, such as with a partner, family member, or friend. We may feel guilty or selfish for wanting to let go of something if it could potentially hurt someone we care about.

For example, someone may be in a toxic friendship but feel responsible for their friend's feelings. They may worry that if they distance themselves or end the friendship, their friend will feel hurt or rejected. This fear of hurting their friend's feelings can cause them to hold onto the friendship even though it's not healthy for them.

It's important to remember that we can't control other people's feelings and are not responsible for them. While it's important to be considerate of others, we also need to prioritize our own well-being and make choices that are in our best interest. Letting go can be difficult, but it's essential for our growth and happiness, and ultimately, our relationships may even improve as a result.

Holding onto past hurts: Holding onto past hurts can be an obstacle in letting go because it keeps us stuck in negative emotions and prevents us from moving forward. It can be difficult to release the pain of past hurts, especially if they were traumatic or deeply impactful. Some people may feel that holding onto the pain is a way to keep themselves safe from future harm, while others may feel that they don't deserve to let go and move on. However, holding onto past hurts can ultimately damage our mental and emotional health and our relationships with others.

When we hold onto past hurts, we may continue to feel angry, resentful, or bitter towards the person or situation that caused the pain. This can lead to feelings of isolation and disconnection from others, as well as difficulty trusting and forming close relationships. Additionally, the negative emotions associated with holding onto past hurts can lead to physical health problems, such as chronic stress and inflammation.

It's important to acknowledge and validate our feelings surrounding past hurts but also to work towards letting go of them. This may involve seeking support from a therapist or trusted friend, practicing self-care and self-compassion, and reframing our thoughts and beliefs about the situation. Letting go of past hurts can lead to greater emotional freedom, improved relationships, and a more positive outlook on life.

Difficulty forgiving oneself: Difficulty forgiving oneself can be a significant obstacle in letting go of negative emotions and experiences. When we hold onto feelings of guilt, shame, or regret, it can be challenging to move forward and make positive changes in our lives. It can be especially difficult to let go when we feel like we've made a mistake or let ourselves down in some way.

Sometimes, we might feel like we don't deserve to let

go and move on from our past actions or experiences. This can lead to a cycle of self-blame and self-criticism that can be hard to break free from. In these situations, practicing self-compassion and recognizing that everyone makes mistakes and has moments of weakness can be helpful.

Forgiving oneself doesn't mean forgetting or excusing past behavior, but it does mean acknowledging that we are human and deserving of self-love and forgiveness. It can be a powerful step towards letting go of negative emotions and creating a more positive and fulfilling life.

Letting go can be challenging, and there are many obstacles that can make it difficult. Guilt and shame can be powerful emotions that prevent us from moving forward and letting go of the past. However, by recognizing these feelings and addressing them, we can begin to release them and create space for growth and transformation. We can overcome these obstacles with self-awareness, patience, and compassion and move towards a more fulfilling and joyful life.

Negative Self-Talk

Negative self-talk can be a significant obstacle to letting go. It involves the critical and often destructive inner voice that tells us we're not good enough, smart enough, or worthy enough to make changes in our lives. This type of self-talk can hold us back from letting go of old patterns, beliefs, and habits. Some specific ways that negative self-talk can impede our ability to let go include:

Self-doubt and self-criticism: Self-doubt and self-criticism are common forms of negative self-talk that can be major obstacles in letting go. When we doubt ourselves or criticize ourselves, we may believe that we're incapable of making positive changes in our lives or that we don't deserve to let go of something holding us back. This can make it difficult to take the necessary steps toward letting go and moving forward.

Self-doubt can take many forms, such as questioning our abilities, second-guessing our decisions, or feeling like an imposter. Self-criticism can involve harshly judging ourselves, dwelling on past mistakes, or constantly comparing ourselves to others. Both self-doubt and self-criticism can lead to a negative self-image and a lack of confidence, which can make it difficult to take action toward letting go.

It's important to recognize and challenge negative self-talk to overcome these obstacles. This may involve practicing self-compassion, reframing negative thoughts into more positive ones, or seeking support from others. By cultivating a more positive and self-affirming mindset, we can better navigate the process of letting go and ultimately move towards a more fulfilling and meaningful life.

Perfectionism: Perfectionism is a common form of negative self-talk that can hinder our ability to let go. When we have unrealistic expectations of ourselves and strive for perfection, we may become paralyzed by fear of failure or not living up to our own high standards. This can prevent us from taking risks, trying new things, and ultimately letting go of what is no longer serving us.

Perfectionism can also lead to a constant state of self-criticism and self-doubt, as we may never feel like we are good enough or have done enough. This can create a cycle of negative self-talk that reinforces our fear of letting go and moving forward. Instead, it's important to recognize that perfection is an unrealistic standard and that we are all human, with flaws and imperfections. By letting go of the need to be perfect, we can embrace our authentic selves and allow ourselves to grow and change.

All-or-nothing thinking: All-or-nothing thinking is a type of negative self-talk that can be an obstacle to letting go. This is the idea that things are either all good or all bad, with no middle ground or nuance. For example, you may think that if you're not perfect at something, then you're a failure. This type of thinking can make it difficult to let go of past mistakes or failures, as it reinforces the belief that anything less than perfection is unacceptable.

All-or-nothing thinking can also make it difficult to make progress toward letting go, as it creates a mindset of extremes. If you can't completely let go of something, then you may feel like you've failed. This can lead to a sense of defeat and make it harder to keep trying.

Learning to recognize all-or-nothing thinking and challenging it with more balanced, realistic thinking can be a helpful tool in letting go. For example, instead of thinking, "I must completely let go of this situation, or I'm a failure," you can reframe it as "Letting go is a process and progress, and even small steps are valuable." This shift in mindset can help you move forward towards letting go rather than feeling stuck in an all-or-nothing mindset.

Catastrophizing: Catastrophizing is another form of

negative self-talk that can be an obstacle in letting go. It's the tendency to imagine the worst possible outcome of a situation and then dwell on it. When we catastrophize, we make the situation seem bigger and more overwhelming than it is, which can make it difficult to let go and move on.

For example, if someone is struggling with a difficult breakup, they may catastrophize and imagine that they'll never find love again or that they're doomed to be alone forever. These thoughts can create a sense of hopelessness and make it hard to let go of the past and move forward.

Catastrophizing can also be related to anxiety, as it often involves worrying about things that are out of our control. It can be challenging to let go of these worries and move on, but recognizing when we're catastrophizing can help us take a step back and reframe our thoughts more positively and realistically.

Dismissing positive experiences: Dismissing positive experiences is another way in which negative self-talk can be an obstacle to letting go. When we hold onto negative thoughts and beliefs, we may discount positive experiences and focus only on the negative. This can make it difficult to see the good things in life and contribute to unhappiness and dissatisfaction.

For example, someone who struggles with negative self-talk may have a great day at work but dismiss it as a fluke and continue to dwell on the mistakes they made earlier in the week. This can make it difficult to let go of past mistakes and move forward with a positive outlook. By recognizing and challenging negative self-talk, we can start to shift our focus toward the positive and learn to appreciate and celebrate the good things in life.

Comparison to others: Comparison to others can be a major obstacle in letting go. When we constantly compare ourselves to others, we may feel like we're not good enough or that we don't measure up. This can create a sense of inadequacy and prevent us from letting go of negative emotions and beliefs.

For example, if we're constantly comparing ourselves to someone who seems to have it all together, we may feel like we're failing in comparison. We may hold onto negative emotions and beliefs about ourselves, such as feeling like we're not smart enough or not successful enough. This can prevent us from taking risks or trying new things and ultimately hold us back from personal growth and transformation.

Additionally, comparing ourselves to others can also lead to jealousy and resentment, which can be toxic emotions to hold onto. It's important to remember that everyone has their own journey and that we are all unique individuals with our own strengths and weaknesses. Comparing ourselves to others only serves to create unnecessary stress and can hinder our ability to let go and move forward in a positive direction.

Fear of failure and rejection: fear of failure and rejection can be a major obstacle in letting go. When we hold onto things that are no longer serving us, it may be because we fear the consequences of letting go. We may worry that if we let go of something and fail, we'll feel like a failure ourselves. Or we may fear rejection from others if we let go of something that they think is important.

This fear can be especially strong when it comes to our relationships. We may hold onto toxic relationships because we fear being alone, or we may stay in a job that is making us unhappy because we fear not being able to find another job. This fear can lead us to stay stuck in situations that are not serving us and prevent us from making positive changes in our lives.

It's important to recognize that failure and rejection are a natural part of life and do not reflect our worth. We can learn and grow from these experiences and use them as opportunities for personal development. It's also important to remember that we can't please everyone and that letting go of something may be the best thing for us, even if it means facing some criticism or disapproval from others.

In conclusion, negative self-talk can be a powerful obstacle in the process of letting go. Our inner dialogue with ourselves can greatly influence our beliefs and behaviors. When we engage in negative self-talk, we reinforce the idea that we cannot change or grow. We limit ourselves and prevent ourselves from moving forward. However, by becoming aware of our negative self-talk and actively working to reframe our thoughts and beliefs, we can begin to break free from this obstacle and move towards a more positive, empowered mindset. Letting go becomes possible when we let go of the negative thoughts that hold us back.

In the following sections, we'll explore some practical techniques for overcoming these obstacles and learning how to let go.

PART II - CHAPTER 9 - PRACTICAL TECHNIQUES FOR LETTING GO

Learning to let go can be challenging, but it is a skill that can be developed with practice. This section and the following chapters will explore practical techniques that can help you let go of negative emotions, attachments, and beliefs. These techniques can be used in a variety of situations, from letting go of a past relationship to releasing the fear of failure. By implementing these techniques, you can experience greater inner peace, improved relationships, and a more fulfilling life.

Letting go can be a challenging and sometimes painful process, but there are several practical techniques that can help. Here are a few:

Letting go of negative emotions, attachments, and beliefs is an essential step toward living a happy and fulfilling life. The techniques discussed in this section provide practical ways to cultivate a more positive mindset and to let go of what's holding you back. Whether you're dealing with stress, anxiety, or a difficult life transition, these techniques can help you navigate your emotions and find a sense of peace and acceptance.

One of the key takeaways from this section is that letting go is a journey that requires patience and self-compassion. It may take time and practice to release something that's not serving you fully, but with the right tools and techniques, you can make significant progress. By focusing on the present moment, practicing gratitude, and reframing negative thoughts, you can cultivate a more positive outlook on life and let go of what's holding you back.

Ultimately, these techniques aim to help you create a more peaceful, happy, and fulfilling life. By letting go of negative emotions, attachments, and beliefs, you can free up space for new experiences and opportunities. So, take the time to practice these techniques and let go of what's holding you back. Your journey towards greater inner peace and happiness starts now.

CHAPTER 10 – JOURNALING

Journaling can be helpful for letting go of negative thoughts and emotions. By writing down your thoughts and feelings in a journal, you can gain insight into your emotions and patterns of thinking. It can also help you identify negative patterns of behavior and thought that are holding you back.

To use journaling as a tool for letting go, start by finding a quiet and comfortable place to write. Write freely and without judgment, allowing your thoughts and emotions to flow onto the page. You may find it helpful to write about a specific situation or emotion that you are struggling with.

As you write, try to be as honest and open with yourself as possible. Don't worry about spelling or grammar; don't judge yourself by your writing. Instead, allow your thoughts and feelings to come out naturally.

Once you have finished writing, take some time to reflect on what you have written. Notice any patterns or themes that emerge and think about what steps you can take to let go of negative thoughts and emotions. This may involve changing your behavior, seeking help from a therapist or counselor, or simply accepting your thoughts and feelings without judgment.

Remember that journaling is a personal and private practice, and you can use it in whatever way feels most helpful to you. Some people find it helpful to write daily, while others prefer to journal only when they are feeling particularly stressed or overwhelmed. Here are a few specific ways that journaling can help with letting go:

Freewriting: Freewriting is a technique used to promote the flow of thoughts and ideas onto paper without inhibition. The goal is to write whatever comes to mind without worrying about grammar, spelling, or punctuation. This technique can be helpful in letting go of negative thoughts and emotions, as it allows for the expression and release of pent-up emotions.

By writing without judgment, you may uncover underlying feelings or beliefs you were unaware of before. This can provide insights into the root of your negative emotions, which can then be addressed and released. Freewriting can also help to increase self-awareness and promote a sense of emotional release and relaxation.

Write a letter: Writing a letter is a form of expressive writing that can be particularly helpful when letting go of negative thoughts and emotions. It allows you to get your thoughts and feelings out on paper and can provide a sense of closure. You may choose to address the letter to a specific person or situation or simply write to yourself. The key is to be honest about your emotions and express what you need to say. This can help you gain clarity and perspective on the situation and can be a powerful step in the process of letting go.

It's important to note that you don't necessarily have to send the letter. In some cases, simply writing it out can be enough to help you let go. However, if you choose to send the letter, it's important to consider the potential consequences and whether it's really in your best interest. It may be helpful to seek a therapist's or trusted friend's guidance to help you decide.

Make a list: Making a list can be a helpful technique for organizing your thoughts and creating a plan of action for letting go.

Here's how you can do it:

Make a list of the things that are holding you back: This can include negative thoughts, emotions, situations, or people that are preventing you from moving forward.

Identify patterns: Look for patterns or common themes in your list. Are there certain thoughts or situations that keep coming up? This can help you identify the root cause of your difficulty in letting go.

Create a second list of actions: Once you have identified the things that are holding you back, create a second list of actions you can take to let go of them. This can include techniques like mindfulness meditation, cognitive-behavioral techniques, journaling, or seeking support from others.

Prioritize your list: Look at your second list and prioritize the actions based on what feels most feasible and effective for you. Start with the actions that feel easiest to implement and work your way up to more challenging techniques.

Take action: Finally, take action on your list. Start with the first action on your list and make a commitment to follow through with it. Celebrate your progress and continue working through your list until you feel that you have successfully let go of what was holding you back.

Reflect on positive experiences: Reflecting on positive experiences is a technique that can help you let go of negative thoughts and emotions. By focusing on positive experiences and accomplishments, you can boost your self-esteem and create a more positive outlook on life.

To use this technique, take time to reflect on positive experiences in your life, such as a job promotion, an achievement in a hobby, or a personal accomplishment. Write down how these experiences made you feel and what positive qualities they brought out in you, such as confidence, joy, or a sense of fulfillment. By doing this, you can shift your focus away from negative thoughts and emotions and start to cultivate a more positive mindset.

Gratitude journaling: Gratitude journaling is a powerful technique that involves regularly writing down things that you are grateful for in your life. It helps to shift your focus from negative thoughts to positive ones and cultivate a sense of appreciation for the good things in your life, no matter how small they may seem. By focusing on the positive, you can create a more positive mindset and develop a greater sense of resilience in the face of challenges.

To get started with gratitude journaling, set aside a few minutes each day to reflect on what you are grateful for. Write down at least three things that you appreciate in your life, no matter how small they may seem. These could be simple things like a good cup of coffee in the morning, the support of a friend, or a beautiful sunset.

It can also be helpful to reflect on why you are grateful for these things. What positive impact have they had on your life? How have they helped you grow or overcome challenges? By reflecting on these questions, you can deepen your sense of appreciation for the good things in your life.

Gratitude journaling doesn't have to be a daily practice, but it can be helpful to incorporate it into your routine on a regular basis. You might choose to journal once a week or every day for a set period of time. The key is making it a habit and approaching it with an open and positive mindset.

Self-reflection: Write about your own behavior, thoughts, and feelings in a non-judgmental way. This can help you identify patterns and gain insight into your own thought processes.

Write affirmations: Writing affirmations is a powerful tool to help you let go of negative thoughts and emotions. Affirmations are positive statements that you repeat to yourself to create a more positive mindset. When you write affirmations, you create a written record of the positive statements you want to focus on. This can be a helpful reminder to return to when you are feeling stuck or negative.

When writing affirmations, it's important to make them personal and specific. Start by identifying the negative thoughts and emotions you want to let go of, then create affirmations that directly counteract them. For example, if you are struggling with self-doubt, you might write an affirmation such as "I am capable and competent."

Using the present tense and avoiding negative language when writing affirmations is important. For example, instead of saying, "I will not be afraid," say, "I am brave and confident." This helps to create a positive mindset and reinforces the idea that positive statements are true in the present moment.

Once you have written your affirmations, it's important to repeat them to yourself on a regular basis. This can be done by reading them aloud, writing them down, or repeating them silently to yourself throughout the day. By focusing on positive affirmations, you can reprogram your mind and create a more positive outlook on life.

Write a goodbye: Writing a goodbye letter is a technique that can help you process your emotions and bring closure to a relationship or situation you are letting go of. In this letter, you can express your feelings and thoughts about the situation, including any unresolved issues or grievances.

Writing a goodbye letter can also provide a sense of closure and allow you to say goodbye on your own terms. Focusing on the positive aspects of the relationship or situation can be helpful while acknowledging any challenges or difficulties. Writing the letter can be cathartic and provide a sense of relief, helping you move forward with greater clarity and purpose.

Creative writing: Creative writing is a powerful tool for processing emotions and exploring your inner world. It can be a cathartic way to express feelings that may be difficult to put into words, and it can help you gain new insights and perspectives on your experiences.

Writing poetry, for example, can allow you to tap into your emotions and create a vivid image of your inner experience. Storytelling, on the other hand, can help you explore different narratives and perspectives on a situation and allow you to step outside of yourself and see things from a different angle. Engaging in creative writing can help you gain clarity and perspective on your thoughts and emotions and provide an outlet for self-expression and exploration. It can also be a fun and enjoyable way to engage with yourself and your inner world.

Goal setting: Goal setting is a powerful technique for letting go of negative thoughts and emotions by focusing on the future. It involves identifying what you want to achieve and creating a plan to get there. By setting goals, you can shift your focus from the past to the present and future. This can help you feel more motivated and positive as you work towards something that is important to you.

To set effective goals, it's important to make them specific, measurable, achievable, relevant, and time-bound (SMART). This means identifying exactly what you want to achieve, breaking it down into manageable steps, and setting a deadline for each step. It's also important to stay flexible and adjust your goals as necessary in response to changes in your life or circumstances.

Setting and working towards goals can create a sense of purpose and direction in your life. This can help you feel more in control and less overwhelmed by negative thoughts and emotions. Ultimately, goal setting can help you let go of the past and create a brighter future for yourself.

CHAPTER 11
– COGNITIVE-
BEHAVIORAL
TECHNIQUES

Cognitive-behavioral techniques are a type of therapy that can be used to help individuals identify and change negative thought patterns and behaviors that may be contributing to stress, anxiety, or other negative emotions. These techniques can be helpful for letting go of negative thoughts and emotions, as they involve addressing the underlying beliefs and behaviors that may be contributing to these feelings.

Cognitive-behavioral therapy typically involves several key components, including:

Identifying negative thought patterns: This involves becoming aware of the thoughts and beliefs that may be contributing to negative emotions. By identifying these negative thought patterns, individuals can begin to challenge and reframe them more positively and helpfully.

Challenging negative beliefs: Once negative thought patterns have been identified, individuals can work on challenging and reframing these beliefs more positively and realistically. This can involve looking for evidence to support or refute these beliefs and developing more positive and helpful self-talk.

Changing negative behaviors: In addition to changing negative thought patterns, cognitive-behavioral therapy may also involve changing negative behaviors that may be contributing to negative emotions. This can involve developing more positive coping strategies, such as exercise or relaxation techniques, or changing patterns of behavior that may be contributing to stress or anxiety.

Overall, cognitive-behavioral techniques can be a helpful way to let go of negative thoughts and emotions by addressing the underlying beliefs and behaviors that may be contributing to these feelings. By identifying negative thought patterns, challenging negative beliefs, and changing negative behaviors, individuals can develop a more positive and balanced approach to life, leading to greater emotional well-being and overall mental health.

Recognize negative self-talk: Negative self-talk refers to the inner dialogue we have with ourselves that is critical, judgmental, and self-defeating. It can hold us back from reaching our full potential and contribute to feelings of anxiety, depression, and low self-esteem. However, by becoming more aware of our negative self-talk, we can begin to challenge and change it.

One way to recognize negative self-talk is to start by identifying the negative thoughts that are holding you back. Keeping a thought journal is a helpful technique for this. In a thought journal, you write down the thoughts and emotions that come up throughout the day and identify any negative patterns or themes. This can help you become more aware of your negative self-talk and its impact on your well-being.

Once you have identified your negative self-talk, you can begin to challenge it. This involves questioning the validity of your negative thoughts and finding evidence to counter them. For example, if you think, "I'm not good enough," ask yourself if that thought is true. Is there evidence to support it, or is it just a self-limiting belief?

You can also reframe your negative self-talk by replacing it with positive affirmations. For example, instead of thinking, "I can't do this," try thinking, "I can do this, and I will try my best." This can help you cultivate a more positive and self-compassionate mindset.

Overall, recognizing and challenging negative self-talk is an important step in letting go of negative thoughts and emotions. By becoming more aware of our inner dialogue and learning to reframe it in a positive way, we can cultivate greater emotional well-being and overall mental health.

Challenge negative thoughts: Negative thoughts can be a major source of stress and anxiety, and they can hold us back from reaching our goals and living a fulfilling life. One effective way to let go of negative thoughts is to challenge them by questioning their validity.

Once you have identified a negative thought, take a moment to examine it and ask yourself if it is really true. For example, if you think, "I'm never going to be able to finish this project," ask yourself if that thought is based on reality or if it is just a self-limiting belief. Is there evidence to support the thought, or is it just an assumption or fear?

Another way to challenge negative thoughts is to consider alternative explanations or perspectives. For example, instead of thinking, "I'm not good enough," consider reframing the thought to "I may not be perfect, but I am doing the best I can." This can help you shift your focus away from self-criticism and towards self-compassion.

It's important to remember that challenging negative thoughts is not about denying or suppressing them but rather about recognizing their impact on our well-being and taking steps to counter them. By questioning the validity of our negative thoughts and reframing them in a more positive light, we can cultivate a more balanced and compassionate mindset and let go of the negative thoughts that hold us back.

Reframe negative thoughts: Reframing negative thoughts is a cognitive-behavioral technique that involves changing the way you think about a situation. It can be particularly useful for letting go of negative thoughts that are holding you back.

Challenging negative thoughts with a more positive or neutral alternative is one way to reframe them. For example, if you find yourself thinking, "I can't do this," try reframing it by saying, "I haven't learned how to do this yet" or "I am in the process of learning how to do this." This reframing can help shift your focus away from self-criticism and towards a growth mindset, which can be a powerful motivator.

Another way to reframe negative thoughts is to focus on the positive aspects of a situation, no matter how small. For example, if you are facing a difficult challenge, focus on the skills or resources you already have rather than dwelling on what you lack. By reframing the situation in a more positive light, you can help reduce your stress and anxiety and feel more empowered to take action.

It's important to note that reframing negative thoughts is not about denying or minimizing the challenges we face but rather about cultivating a more balanced and positive perspective. By letting go of negative self-talk and focusing on positive alternatives, we can build resilience and find new opportunities for growth and development.

Practice self-compassion: Practicing self-compassion is a powerful way to let go of negative self-talk and build greater resilience in the face of challenges.

Self-compassion involves treating yourself with kindness and understanding, even when you are facing difficulties or setbacks. Instead of criticizing or judging yourself harshly, try to offer yourself the same kindness and support you would offer a close friend.

One way to practice self-compassion is to start by acknowledging your feelings and experiences with honesty and openness. This means accepting that you are human and that everyone makes mistakes and experiences setbacks from time to time. By acknowledging and accepting your feelings, you can begin to let go of self-criticism and start to cultivate a more positive and self-compassionate mindset.

Another way to practice self-compassion is to be mindful of your self-talk. Try to notice when you are being overly critical or judgmental towards yourself and replace these negative thoughts with more positive and self-affirming ones. For example, if you think, "I'm such a failure," try reframing this thought by saying, "I'm doing my best, and that's all I can do right now."

Finally, it's important to remember that self-compassion is not about making excuses or avoiding responsibility for your actions. Rather, it's about treating yourself with the same kindness and understanding that you would offer to a friend, even when you are facing difficult challenges. By practicing self-compassion, you can let go of negative self-talk and build greater resilience and self-confidence in the face of adversity.

Use positive affirmations: Positive affirmations can be a helpful tool to combat negative self-talk and improve self-esteem. They are statements that are designed to challenge negative beliefs and replace them with positive ones. When using positive affirmations, it's important to choose statements that are meaningful and relevant to your situation.

To use positive affirmations effectively, try the following:

Identify the negative belief: Start by identifying the negative belief or thought that you want to replace. For example, if you tend to think, "I'm not good enough," that could be the negative belief you want to address.

Choose a positive affirmation: Choose a positive statement that challenges the negative belief. For example, "I am worthy and capable of achieving my goals."

Repeat the affirmation: Repeat the positive affirmation to yourself several times a day, either silently or out loud. This helps to reinforce the positive message and replace the negative belief.

Believe in the affirmation: It's important to believe in the positive affirmation and the message it conveys. Try to imagine yourself as the person described in the affirmation and visualize yourself living according to that statement.

Remember that positive affirmations are not a magic solution, but they can be a helpful tool in building self-confidence and combatting negative self-talk. It may take time and practice to use positive affirmations regularly, but the benefits can be significant.

Use visualization: Visualization is a technique that involves creating mental images or scenarios to promote relaxation and positive emotions. To use visualization for letting go, you can start by finding a quiet and comfortable space to sit or lie down. Close your eyes and take a few deep breaths to relax your body and mind.

Then, imagine a situation or scenario in which you are holding onto negative thoughts or emotions. Visualize yourself acknowledging these thoughts and emotions, but also visualize yourself letting them go. Imagine them floating away from you like balloons or being swept away by a river. You can also visualize yourself replacing these negative thoughts and emotions with positive ones, such as feelings of gratitude, joy, or contentment.

Visualization can be a powerful tool for creating a sense

of calm and control in difficult situations. Regular practice can help you cultivate a more positive mindset and let go of negative thoughts and emotions.

Take action: Taking action is crucial in letting go of negative thoughts and emotions. After identifying and challenging negative thoughts, it's important to take concrete steps to move forward. This may involve changing your behavior in some way, such as setting boundaries or taking a break from a stressful situation. It could also mean taking steps to address the root cause of the negative thoughts and emotions, such as seeking therapy or making lifestyle changes.

By taking action, you're letting go of negative thoughts and emotions and empowering yourself to create positive change in your life. Remember to be patient and kind to yourself throughout the process, as letting go of negative thoughts and emotions can take time and effort.

In conclusion, cognitive-behavioral techniques can be effective tools for helping individuals let go of negative thought patterns and behaviors that may be holding them back. By working with a therapist to identify and challenge negative thoughts, individuals can learn to reframe their thinking and develop more positive coping mechanisms. Additionally, recognizing and replacing negative behaviors with more positive ones can lead to increased self-esteem and greater control over one's life. With the help of cognitive-behavioral techniques, individuals can learn to let go of past hurts and move forward in a positive direction.

Remember that cognitive-behavioral techniques take practice and patience. Be gentle with yourself and take things one step at a time.

CHAPTER 12 - MINDFULNESS MEDITATION

Mindfulness meditation is a powerful technique for letting go of negative thoughts and emotions. It involves training your mind to focus on the present moment rather than dwelling on the past or worrying about the future. This can help you develop greater awareness of your thoughts and emotions and cultivate a more balanced and accepting approach to life.

During mindfulness meditation, you sit in a comfortable position and focus your attention on your breath, body, or another point of focus. As thoughts or emotions arise, you simply observe them without judgment and gently guide your attention back to your point of focus. Over time, this practice can help you develop greater clarity and focus and greater acceptance of your thoughts and emotions.

Research has shown that mindfulness meditation can effectively reduce stress, anxiety, and depression and improve overall mental health and well-being. By cultivating greater awareness of your thoughts and emotions, you can begin to let go of negative patterns of thought and behavior and develop a more positive and accepting approach to life.

Overall, mindfulness meditation can be a powerful technique for letting go of negative thoughts and emotions and developing greater awareness and acceptance of the present moment. This technique can help you cultivate greater emotional well-being and overall mental health with practice.

Here are a few specific ways that mindfulness meditation can help with letting go:

Focus on the present moment: The present moment is where life unfolds, and cultivating an awareness of the present moment can help individuals let go of distracting thoughts and emotions and cultivate a sense of inner peace and well-being. During mindfulness meditation, the goal is to observe the present moment without judgment, simply noticing the sensations, thoughts, and emotions that arise without getting caught up in them.

When you find yourself dwelling on the past or worrying about the future during meditation, you can use various techniques to bring your focus back to the present moment. One technique is to focus on your breath, noticing the sensation of the breath moving in and out of your body. You can also focus on the physical sensations in your body, such as the feeling of your feet on the ground or the sensation of your hands on your lap.

Another technique is to notice your thoughts and emotions without judgment, simply acknowledging their presence and then redirecting your attention back to the present moment. For example, if you find yourself worrying about something in the future, you can acknowledge the worry without judgment and then bring your attention back to your breath or the present moment.

By focusing on the present moment during mindfulness meditation, individuals can train their minds to be more present and less distracted by thoughts and emotions. This can lead to a greater sense of inner peace, happiness, and well-being in daily life.

Observe your thoughts and emotions: Observing your thoughts and emotions is a key aspect of mindfulness meditation. As you meditate, you may notice that your mind starts to wander or that certain thoughts or emotions come up. The goal of mindfulness meditation is not to eliminate these thoughts and emotions but rather to observe them without judgment.

Observing your thoughts and emotions without judgment creates a sense of distance between yourself and your thoughts and emotions. This can help you avoid getting caught up in them or reacting to them in a negative way. Instead, you can simply notice them and let them pass without getting attached to them.

One way to practice observing your thoughts and emotions is to simply bring your attention to your breath and then notice any thoughts or emotions that come up. You might notice that your mind starts wandering or feeling anxious or frustrated. Instead of trying to push these thoughts or emotions away, simply observe them and let them pass.

It's important to note that observing your thoughts and emotions without judgment doesn't mean that you should ignore or suppress them. Rather, it means acknowledging them and allowing them to be present without getting caught up in them. This can help you cultivate a greater sense of emotional resilience and well-being.

Overall, observing your thoughts and emotions during mindfulness meditation can help you cultivate a greater sense of mindfulness and emotional awareness. By noticing your thoughts and emotions without judgment, you can avoid getting caught up in them and cultivate a greater sense of inner peace and well-being.

Practice self-compassion: Self-compassion is a key aspect of mindfulness meditation. It involves approaching yourself with kindness and understanding rather than criticizing or judging yourself for your thoughts and emotions.

When you practice self-compassion during mindfulness meditation, you create a safe and supportive space for yourself.

This can help you feel more relaxed and less stressed, which can positively impact your overall well-being.

One way to practice self-compassion during mindfulness meditation is to acknowledge your thoughts and emotions without judgment simply. If you notice that you're feeling anxious or stressed, for example, you might say to yourself, "It's okay to feel this way. This is a normal human experience."

It's also important to be gentle with yourself during mindfulness meditation. If you find that your mind is wandering or you're feeling distracted, try not to judge or criticize yourself. Instead, simply bring your attention back to your breath or chosen focus point and continue meditating.

Another way to practice self-compassion during mindfulness meditation is to use positive affirmations or self-talk. For example, you might say to yourself, "I am doing the best I can" or "I am worthy of love and compassion."

Practicing self-compassion during mindfulness meditation can help you cultivate greater self-awareness and emotional well-being. By approaching yourself with kindness and understanding, you can create a safe and supportive space for yourself to grow and develop.

Use breathing techniques: Using breathing techniques is a common and effective way to stay present during mindfulness meditation. Focusing on your breath can be a helpful way to stay grounded in the present moment and anchor your attention, which can help reduce distracting thoughts and emotions.

There are a variety of breathing techniques that you can use during mindfulness meditation. One simple technique is to focus on the sensation of your breath moving in and out of your body. This involves paying attention to the physical sensation of your breath as it moves through your nostrils and into your lungs.

Another breathing technique is to count your breaths. This involves counting each inhale and exhaling up to a certain number, such as 10, and then starting again at one. This technique can help you stay focused on your breath and stay present in the moment.

More advanced breathing techniques, such as deep belly breathing or alternate nostril breathing, can further deepen your mindfulness practice. These techniques can help you relax and focus your attention more deeply, which can lead to a greater sense of calm and inner peace.

Overall, using breathing techniques during mindfulness meditation can be a powerful way to stay present in the moment and reduce distracting thoughts and emotions. By focusing on your breath, you can cultivate a greater sense of mindfulness and emotional awareness, which can positively impact your overall well-being.

Cultivate awareness of your body: Cultivating awareness of your body is an important aspect of mindfulness meditation. By paying attention to physical sensations in your body, such as tension or discomfort, you can develop a greater sense of self-awareness and learn to release physical tension that may be contributing to stress or anxiety.

One way to cultivate awareness of your body during mindfulness meditation is to simply tune in to physical sensations. Close your eyes and focus on the feeling of your feet on the floor, the weight of your body in your chair, or the sensations in your hands or face.

As you do this, you may notice areas of tension or discomfort in your body. Use mindfulness techniques, such as deep breathing or progressive muscle relaxation, to release any physical tension and bring yourself back to a state of relaxation.

Progressive muscle relaxation involves tensing and then releasing each muscle group in your body, one at a time, while focusing on the physical sensations. This technique can help you release physical tension and promote greater relaxation.

Deep breathing, as mentioned earlier, involves taking

slow, deep breaths and focusing on the sensation of your breath moving in and out of your body. This technique can help you calm your mind and reduce physical tension and stress.

By cultivating awareness of your body during mindfulness meditation, you can learn to release physical tension and promote a greater sense of relaxation and well-being. This can have a positive impact on your overall mental and emotional health.

Use guided meditations: Guided meditations are a helpful way to get started with mindfulness meditation, particularly if you're new to the practice. Guided meditations typically involve an instructor or audio recording that provides verbal guidance to help you stay focused and relaxed during meditation.

There are many apps and websites that offer free guided meditations, making it easy to find a guided meditation that suits your needs and preferences. These guided meditations may focus on different themes, such as relaxation, stress relief, or self-compassion, and may range in length from just a few minutes to an hour or more.

In addition to online resources, you can also attend a meditation class or workshop to receive in-person guidance and support. Many yoga studios, community centers, and spiritual organizations offer meditation classes or workshops that are open to the public.

Using guided meditations during mindfulness meditation can be particularly helpful for beginners, as it provides structure and support for your practice. Guided meditations can help you stay focused and relaxed and inspire and motivate your meditation practice.

Overall, using guided meditations during mindfulness meditation can be a helpful way to get started with the practice, particularly if you're new to meditation or struggling to establish a regular practice on your own. By using guided meditations, you can learn to stay present in the moment and develop a greater sense of mindfulness and emotional awareness.

In conclusion, mindfulness meditation is a powerful tool for reducing stress, anxiety, and negative emotions and increasing feelings of calm and well-being. By practicing mindfulness regularly, we can learn to stay present in the moment, let go of worries about the past or future, and cultivate a more positive and compassionate outlook on life. There are many different forms of mindfulness meditation, from body scans and loving-kindness meditations to breath-focused practices and walking meditations. Experiment with different techniques and find the ones that most resonate with you. With consistent practice, mindfulness meditation can help you live a more mindful, intentional, and fulfilling life.

Remember, mindfulness meditation is a practice, so it's important to approach it with patience and consistency. With time and practice, you may find that it becomes easier to let go of negative thoughts and emotions and focus on the present moment.

CHAPTER 13 - VISUALIZATION EXERCISES

Visualization exercises are a powerful technique for letting go of negative thoughts and emotions by helping you to focus on positive outcomes. They involve using your imagination to create a vivid mental image of a desired outcome or situation. This can include imagining yourself succeeding at a task, achieving a goal, or overcoming a challenge. By visualizing these positive outcomes, you can create a more positive mindset and shift your focus away from negative thoughts and emotions.

To practice visualization, find a quiet place where you can sit comfortably without distractions. Close your eyes and imagine the desired outcome or scenario in as much detail as possible. Use all your senses to create a vivid mental image, including the sights, sounds, smells, and feelings associated with the situation.

As you visualize the outcome, try to experience the emotions associated with it. Feel the sense of joy, accomplishment, or contentment that comes with achieving your goal. Allow yourself to experience these positive emotions fully.

Visualization exercises can be particularly effective when used in conjunction with other techniques, such as goal setting or positive affirmations. By visualizing your desired outcome and affirming your belief in your ability to achieve it, you can create a powerful combination that helps you to let go of negative thoughts and emotions and focus on the positive. Here are a few specific visualization exercises that can help with letting go:

Letting go visualization: Letting go visualization is a mindfulness exercise that can help you release negative emotions or beliefs that are holding you back. It involves visualizing yourself letting go of these negative thoughts and feelings and allowing yourself to move forward with greater peace and clarity.

To practice this technique, find a quiet and comfortable place where you can sit or lie down without interruption. Close your eyes and take a few deep breaths, focusing on the sensation of the air moving in and out of your body.

Next, visualize the negative thought or emotion that you want to let go of. See it as a physical object or symbol representing that thought or emotion. Hold that image in your mind for a moment.

Now, imagine yourself physically letting go of that object or symbol. You might imagine yourself dropping it or releasing it into the wind. Whatever feels most natural to you.

As you release the object or symbol, visualize the negative thought or emotion dissipating into the distance. See it disappear from your life and feel a sense of relief and release.

Finally, take a few deep breaths and allow yourself to feel a sense of calm and peace. Take note of any sensations or feelings that arise and allow yourself to bask in this sense of release and freedom.

With regular practice, this technique can help you develop greater mindfulness and awareness and cultivate a deeper sense of inner peace and clarity.

Future visualization: This exercise involves visualizing a positive outcome or scenario in the future and imagining yourself letting go of any negative thoughts or emotions that might be holding you back.

Gratitude visualization: Gratitude visualization is a powerful tool for letting go of negative thoughts and emotions and focusing on the positive aspects of your life. To practice gratitude visualization, find a quiet and comfortable place to sit or lie down. Close your eyes and take a few deep breaths, allowing yourself to relax and let go of any tension or stress.

Next, start to visualize everything you're grateful for in your life. This could be anything from the people in your life to the experiences you've had to the things you own. Allow yourself to feel a sense of gratitude and appreciation for these things and try to imagine them in as much detail as possible.

For example, if you're grateful for your friends, picture yourself spending time with them, laughing, and having fun. If you're grateful for your health, imagine yourself feeling strong and energetic. If you're grateful for your home, visualize the rooms and the things inside them.

As you visualize these things, allow yourself to feel the positive emotions that come with gratitude, such as joy, love, and contentment. Let go of any negative thoughts or emotions that may be holding you back and focus on the abundance and positivity in your life. When you're ready, slowly open your eyes and return to the present moment, feeling refreshed and renewed.

Practice self-compassion: Practicing self-compassion is an important aspect of letting go. When we hold onto negative thoughts or emotions, we often criticize ourselves and may feel like we're not good enough. However, self-compassion involves treating ourselves with kindness and understanding, just as we would with a friend. This means acknowledging our feelings without judgment or criticism and recognizing that everyone makes mistakes and experiences setbacks.

It also involves giving ourselves permission to take the time and space we need to heal and move forward. By practicing self-compassion, we can let go of self-blame and self-doubt and instead cultivate a sense of kindness and acceptance towards ourselves.

Seek support: Seeking support from others can be an important part of the letting go process. Talking to friends, family, or a therapist can help you gain new perspectives, receive emotional validation, and feel less alone in your journey. A therapist can provide additional guidance and support and can help you develop healthy coping mechanisms to deal with difficult emotions that may arise during the letting go process.

It's important to remember that seeking support is a sign of strength, not weakness. Letting go can be a challenging and emotional process, and having someone to talk to can make all the difference. Additionally, seeking support from others can help you feel less isolated and remind you that you're not alone in your struggles. Whether it's a trusted friend, family member, or mental health professional, don't be afraid to reach out for support if needed.

Focus on what you can control: Focusing on what you can control is an important aspect of letting go, as it helps shift your focus away from negative thoughts and emotions that can be overwhelming and unproductive. Instead of getting caught up in what you can't change, you can direct your energy towards the things that you do have power over. This might involve setting goals, taking actionable steps towards them, or simply taking care of your physical and mental health.

By taking control of what you can, you can feel a greater sense of agency and empowerment and let go of the things that are outside your control. Additionally, this practice can help you build resilience and adaptability as you learn to navigate challenging situations with a sense of purpose and direction.

Be patient: Being patient is an important aspect of the letting go process. It's easy to feel frustrated or discouraged when we don't see immediate results, but it's important to remember that letting go is a journey, not a destination. It's a process that requires time, effort, and dedication.

When we're trying to let go of something that's holding us back, it's important to recognize that change doesn't happen overnight. It may take several attempts, setbacks, and challenges before we're able to let go fully. It's important to be patient and kind to ourselves during this process.

One way to practice patience is to set realistic expectations for ourselves. We can break down our goals into smaller, more achievable steps and focus on making progress one step at a time. By celebrating our small victories and acknowledging our progress, we can stay motivated and patient as we work towards letting go.

Another way to practice patience is to cultivate a sense of mindfulness and present-moment awareness. By focusing on the present moment and observing our thoughts and emotions without judgment, we can cultivate a sense of calm and acceptance, which can help us be more patient with ourselves and our progress.

In summary, being patient is a key aspect of the letting go process. It allows us to acknowledge that change takes time and effort and helps us stay motivated and focused on our goals. By setting realistic expectations and cultivating mindfulness, we can practice patience and find greater peace and happiness in the letting go process.

Visualization exercises can be powerful tools for letting go of negative thoughts and emotions and for creating a more positive mindset. By visualizing a desired outcome or letting go of something that's holding us back, we can reprogram our minds and find greater peace and happiness. These exercises can take many forms, from gratitude visualizations to letting go visualizations, and can be tailored to individual needs and preferences.

Incorporating visualization exercises into a daily routine, along with other techniques such as mindfulness and self-care, can be an effective way to let go of the past and focus on the present and future. Whether it's imagining a positive outcome, visualizing yourself letting go of a negative belief or emotion, or simply focusing on the things you're grateful for, visualization exercises can help us cultivate a more positive and hopeful outlook on life.

CHAPTER 14 - GRATITUDE PRACTICE

Gratitude practice is a powerful tool for letting go of negative emotions and focusing on the positive aspects of our lives. It involves intentionally focusing on things in your life that you are grateful for and expressing gratitude for them. This practice can help shift our mindset from scarcity and negativity to abundance and positivity.

One way to practice gratitude is to keep a gratitude journal, where you write down a list of things you are grateful for each day. Another way is to practice gratitude in the moment by taking time to appreciate the good things in your life as they happen.

The benefits of gratitude practice include increased feelings of happiness and well-being, improved relationships, and a greater sense of resilience in the face of challenges. By focusing on the positive aspects of our lives, we can let go of negative emotions and cultivate a more positive mindset, leading to greater peace and happiness in our lives.

Here are a few specific gratitude practice techniques that can help with letting go:

Gratitude journaling: Gratitude journaling is a simple yet powerful technique for letting go of negative emotions and cultivating a positive mindset. It involves taking time each day to reflect on and write down things you are grateful for in your life, no matter how small they may seem. By consciously focusing on the positive aspects of your life, you can shift your perspective and create a more positive mindset.

To practice gratitude journaling, set aside a few minutes each day to reflect on your day and identify three things you are grateful for. These can be anything from the people in your life to your experiences or even simple pleasures like a beautiful sunset or a warm cup of tea. Write these things down in a journal or notebook and take a few moments to really savor the feeling of gratitude for each one.

Over time, this practice can help train your mind to focus on the positive and let go of negative thoughts and emotions. It can also help you feel more connected to the good things in your life and cultivate a sense of abundance and joy.

Gratitude letters: Gratitude letters can be a powerful tool for cultivating gratitude and letting go of negative emotions. By expressing gratitude and appreciation for someone else, we can shift our focus from negative thoughts to positive ones. Writing a gratitude letter can also help us feel more connected to others and improve our relationships.

To write a gratitude letter, start by choosing someone you're grateful for. This could be a friend, family member, coworker, or anyone who has positively impacted your life. Then, write a letter expressing your gratitude and thanks. Be specific about what this person has done that you're grateful for and how their actions have affected you. Take time to really reflect on your feelings and express them in a heartfelt way.

You can choose to send the letter or keep it for yourself as a personal reminder of what you're grateful for. Either way, the act of writing the letter can help shift your mindset and let go of negative emotions. It's a simple but powerful practice that can greatly impact your overall well-being.

Gratitude meditation: Gratitude meditation is a technique that involves focusing your attention on the things in your life that you're grateful for. To begin, find a quiet and comfortable place to sit or lie down. Close your eyes and take a few deep breaths to relax your body and mind. Then, start to think about the things you're thankful for in your life, whether it's a supportive friend, a comfortable home, or good health.

As you focus on each thing you're grateful for, try to bring as much detail as possible to mind. Think about how it makes you feel and why you're thankful for it. You may also want to repeat a simple gratitude affirmation, such as "I am grateful for all the blessings in my life" or "I am thankful for the people and experiences that bring joy to my life."

During meditation, it's common for the mind to wander or for negative thoughts and emotions to arise. When this happens, try to acknowledge those thoughts without judgment and then gently bring your attention back to the things you're grateful for.

Gratitude meditation can be practiced for as little or as long as you'd like. Some people prefer to set a timer for a certain amount of time, while others simply meditate until they feel ready to stop. Over time, regularly practicing gratitude meditation can help cultivate a more positive mindset and reduce stress and anxiety.

Gratitude walks: Gratitude walks involve taking a leisurely stroll outside and intentionally focusing on the things in your surroundings that you're grateful for. This can include the natural beauty of the environment, the kindness of strangers or friends, or the small pleasures in life that we often take for granted.

As you walk, pay attention to your surroundings, and take deep breaths to calm your mind and connect with the present moment. You can also try silently expressing gratitude for each thing you observe or think about. This practice can help you cultivate a sense of appreciation and positivity, reduce stress and anxiety, and improve your overall well-being.

Gratitude jar: A gratitude jar is a simple and effective way to practice gratitude on a daily basis. Start by finding a jar or container and some small pieces of paper. Write down something you're grateful for each day on a piece of paper and place it in the jar. You can write down anything that comes to mind, whether it's something big or small.

Over time, the jar will fill up with positive thoughts and memories; you can look back on them whenever you need a reminder of the good things in your life. The act of writing down what you're grateful for and physically putting it in the jar can also help reinforce the feeling of gratitude in your mind and body.

Gratitude sharing: Gratitude sharing is a practice that involves sharing something you are grateful for with others. This practice can be done with family, friends, or a partner, and it can help strengthen your relationships and increase feelings of connectedness.

By sharing your gratitude with others, you can also inspire them to focus on the positive aspects of their lives. This can create a positive feedback loop, where everyone benefits from the increased feelings of gratitude and positivity. The practice of gratitude sharing can be done in many ways, such as sharing during family dinner or before bed, or even through a group chat or phone call with loved ones who are far away.

Gratitude rituals: Gratitude rituals are practices that help us cultivate gratitude on a regular basis. They can be small, simple acts or more elaborate practices that incorporate different elements. The key is to find a ritual that resonates with you and that you can commit to regularly.

One example of a gratitude ritual is saying a gratitude prayer or affirmation before bed or in the morning. This can help set the tone for the day or allow you to reflect on the positive things that happened during the day.

Another example is creating a gratitude altar, where you place objects that represent the things you're grateful for, such as photos or symbols. This can serve as a visual reminder of the good things in your life. Gratitude journaling can also be incorporated into a daily ritual, such as writing down three things you're grateful for each morning or evening. The key is to make the ritual meaningful and enjoyable so that you're motivated to continue it over time.

In conclusion, cultivating gratitude can be a powerful tool in promoting emotional well-being and happiness. By focusing on the positive aspects of our lives and expressing appreciation for them, we can shift our mindset towards positivity and let go of negative emotions. Gratitude can be practiced in many ways, such as journaling, letter writing, or meditation. Making gratitude a daily or weekly habit can significantly impact our mental health and overall happiness and can help us build stronger relationships with others. By prioritizing gratitude, we can learn to appreciate the small joys in life and find greater meaning and purpose.

Remember, incorporating gratitude into your life is about creating a habit of focusing on the positive and appreciating the good things in your life. Find the best gratitude practice for you and make it a regular part of your routine.

CHAPTER 15 - SELF-CARE

Self-care is a vital component of letting go of stress and negative emotions. Taking care of ourselves physically and emotionally can help us feel better and more in control of our lives. One important aspect of self-care is exercise. Exercise releases endorphins, which are natural mood boosters that can help reduce stress and anxiety. Even a short walk or gentle stretching can help clear your mind and improve your mood.

Another aspect of self-care is healthy eating. Eating a balanced diet that's rich in whole foods and nutrients can help support both physical and emotional health. Certain foods, such as those high in omega-3 fatty acids or tryptophan, have been shown to have mood-boosting effects. On the other hand, processed and sugary foods can cause spikes in blood sugar that can leave you feeling tired and irritable.

Getting enough sleep is also crucial for self-care. Lack of sleep can exacerbate stress and negative emotions, making it harder to let go of them. Aim for 7-9 hours of sleep each night and try to establish a consistent sleep schedule to help regulate your body's internal clock.

Other forms of self-care can include taking time to do things you enjoy, spending time with loved ones, and seeking out activities that promote relaxation and stress reduction, such as meditation or yoga. By taking care of ourselves physically and emotionally, we can build resilience and strength that helps us better manage stress and let go of negative emotions.

Here are a few specific self-care techniques that can help with letting go:

Engage in physical self-care: Engaging in physical self-care is an important aspect of overall self-care and can help you let go of stress and negative emotions. Eating a well-balanced diet can provide your body with the nutrients it needs to function properly, which can improve your mood and energy levels. Exercise is also a powerful way to release tension and boost your mood, as it can trigger the release of endorphins, which are natural mood boosters.

Additionally, getting enough sleep is crucial for both physical and emotional health, as it allows your body and mind to rest and recharge. Physical self-care can also help you feel more confident and comfortable in your body, improving your overall well-being.

Prioritize mental self-care: Prioritizing mental self-care is essential to letting go of negative thoughts and emotions. It's important to take time to care for your mental and emotional health, just as you would care for your physical health.

Here are some techniques for mental self-care to consider:

Practice mindfulness: Mindfulness meditation can help you focus on the present moment and let go of negative thoughts and emotions. Mindfulness-based stress reduction (MBSR) has been shown to effectively reduce stress and improve emotional well-being.

Seek therapy: A mental health professional can help you work through emotional issues and develop healthy coping mechanisms for dealing with stress and negative emotions.

Practice self-compassion: Treat yourself with kindness and understanding and avoid self-criticism or self-blame. It's okay to make mistakes or have setbacks, and it's important to be kind and forgiving towards yourself.

Engage in hobbies or activities you enjoy: Participating in activities you find enjoyable can help reduce stress and improve mood.

Connect with others: Building and maintaining healthy relationships can help provide support and reduce feelings of isolation or loneliness.

Take breaks when needed: It's important to take them when you feel overwhelmed or stressed. This can involve taking a short walk, practicing deep breathing, or engaging in a relaxation exercise.

Overall, prioritizing mental self-care can help you build resilience, reduce stress, and let go of negative thoughts and emotions.

Practice self-compassion: Practicing self-compassion is an important aspect of self-care and letting go. It involves treating yourself with the same kindness, understanding, and care you would offer a close friend. This means being gentle with yourself and recognizing that everyone makes mistakes and has weaknesses.

Self-compassion can help you let go of negative self-talk and feelings of shame or guilt, which can hold you back from fully letting go of negative thoughts and emotions. Some ways to practice self-compassion include practicing positive self-talk, forgiving yourself for past mistakes, and focusing on self-care activities that bring you joy and fulfillment.

By treating yourself with kindness and compassion, you can create a more positive and nurturing relationship with yourself and let go of the negative emotions that are holding you back.

Engage in activities you enjoy: Engaging in activities that you enjoy can be an important aspect of self-care and letting go of negative emotions. These activities can provide a sense of pleasure and joy and can help to distract you from negative thoughts or emotions. When you engage in activities that you enjoy, you may feel more energized, motivated, and positive.

It's important to make time for activities you enjoy regularly and prioritize them in your schedule. This can involve setting aside time each day or week for a particular activity or making a conscious effort to incorporate enjoyable activities into your daily routine.

In addition to providing a sense of pleasure, engaging in activities you enjoy can also have other benefits. For example, physical activities like yoga or running can improve your physical health, while creative activities like painting or writing can improve your mental health. Social activities like spending time with friends or volunteering can improve your sense of connection and well-being. Ultimately, engaging in activities you enjoy can help you feel more fulfilled and content and can contribute to a more positive mindset overall.

Set boundaries: Setting boundaries is an important part of self-care and letting go of negative emotions. It involves identifying what activities, people, or situations may be causing stress or anxiety and creating limits around them. This can include setting limits on how much time you spend with certain people, saying no to activities that are not aligned with your values or goals, or creating a schedule that prioritizes self-care activities.

By setting boundaries, you prioritize your own needs and well-being and create a space where you can let go of negative emotions and focus on what's important to you. It can also help you feel more in control of your life and reduce feelings of overwhelm or stress. Remember that setting boundaries may not always be easy, but it is an important step in taking care of yourself and letting go of what no longer serves you.

Take breaks: Taking breaks is an important aspect of self-care, especially when you're feeling overwhelmed or stressed. It can be tempting to push through and keep working, but taking a break can help you be more productive and efficient in the long run.

Some ways to take breaks include going for a walk outside, doing a quick meditation or breathing exercise, or taking a short nap. The key is disconnecting from work or stressors and allowing your mind and body to relax and recharge.

By taking regular breaks, you can reduce stress and increase your overall well-being.

Practice mindfulness: Practicing mindfulness can be a powerful way to engage in self-care and let go of stress and negative emotions. Mindfulness involves bringing your full attention to the present moment without judgment and observing your thoughts and emotions as they arise. It can help you become more aware of your physical and emotional sensations and allow you to respond to them in a calm and non-reactive way.

There are many ways to practice mindfulness, including meditation, mindful breathing, body scanning, and mindful walking. Mindfulness can also be integrated into everyday activities, such as washing dishes or taking a shower, by bringing your full attention to the sensory experience of the activity.

By practicing mindfulness regularly, you can develop a greater sense of calm and clarity and become better equipped to let go of negative thoughts and emotions.

Connect with others: Connecting with others is an important aspect of self-care as it can provide a sense of community, belonging, and support. Social support has been shown to have many benefits for mental health, including reducing symptoms of depression and anxiety, improving self-esteem, and increasing resilience.

There are many ways to connect with others, including joining a club or organization that interests you, attending social events, or reaching out to friends and family members for a conversation or outing. You can also consider joining a support group or seeking professional counseling or therapy to help you work through any emotional challenges you may be facing.

Remember that social connections don't have to be face-to-face, especially in today's digital age. You can also connect with others online through social media or online forums, as long as you prioritize healthy communication and boundaries.

Engage in hobbies and interests: Engaging in hobbies and interests is an important aspect of self-care and can help you let go of stress and negative emotions. Hobbies provide a sense of accomplishment and enjoyment and can help you develop new skills and interests. Engaging in hobbies and interests can also provide a sense of purpose, which can be especially helpful during challenging times.

Some examples of hobbies and interests include playing sports, painting or drawing, cooking, gardening, reading, writing, or playing music. The key is finding activities you enjoy and providing a sense of meaning and purpose to your life. Engaging in hobbies and interests can create a sense of balance in your life and let go of stress and negative emotions.

Practice good self-talk: Practicing good self-talk is an important aspect of self-care. Negative self-talk can fuel feelings of self-doubt, anxiety, and depression, making it harder to let go of negative emotions. To combat this, it's important to challenge negative self-talk and replace it with positive affirmations and self-compassionate statements.

This can be done by noticing when negative thoughts arise and actively questioning their validity. Ask yourself if the negative thought is based on facts or just an assumption and if there is evidence to support the thought. Once you've challenged the negative thought, try replacing it with a positive affirmation or a self-compassionate statement.

For example, instead of thinking, "I'm not good enough,"

try thinking, "I am capable and worthy of love and success." By practicing good self-talk, you can improve your self-esteem and increase your ability to let go of negative emotions.

In conclusion, self-care is an important aspect of letting go and moving forward in life. Taking care of ourselves physically and emotionally can help us let go of stress and negative emotions and improve our overall well-being. Engaging in activities we enjoy, setting boundaries, and practicing good self-talk are just a few examples of self-care practices that can help us let go of the past and focus on the present and future. It's important to prioritize self-care in our daily lives and seek support from others when needed. By prioritizing self-care, we can let go of the things holding us back and live happier, healthier life.

CHAPTER 16 – FORGIVENESS

Practicing forgiveness involves letting go of the anger, resentment, or hurt that you may be holding towards others or yourself. It is important to note that forgiveness is not about condoning or excusing harmful behavior, but rather it is about freeing yourself from the negative emotions that come with holding onto grudges.

One way to practice forgiveness is to start by acknowledging the hurt that was caused. This can involve writing down your thoughts and feelings or talking to a trusted friend or therapist. Once you have acknowledged the hurt, try to understand the other person's perspective and their reasons for their actions. This doesn't mean that you must agree with them or condone their behavior; rather, it can help you see things from a different angle.

Next, make a conscious decision to forgive. This may involve letting go of any desire for revenge or punishment and choosing to focus on moving forward. It can be helpful to use self-compassionate statements, such as "I forgive you, and I release this anger and hurt," or "I deserve peace and happiness, and holding onto this anger is not helping me."

Finally, take steps towards healing and letting go. This may involve practicing self-care, engaging in activities that bring you joy, and seeking support from friends or a therapist if needed. Remember that forgiveness is a journey, and it may take time and effort, but the benefits of letting go of anger and resentment can lead to greater peace, happiness, and overall well-being.

Here are a few specific forgiveness techniques that can help with letting go:

Identify what needs to be forgiven: Identifying what needs to be forgiven is an essential step in the forgiveness process. It involves reflecting on the situation that needs forgiveness, acknowledging your feelings, and identifying what caused them. It's important to be honest with yourself about your emotions and the impact the situation has had on you. Sometimes it may be helpful to write down your thoughts and feelings in a journal, which can help bring clarity to the situation and the forgiveness process.

Once you have identified what needs to be forgiven, the next step is to work on letting go of anger and resentment towards the situation or person. This can be a difficult step, but it's essential to forgiveness. One way to do this is to practice empathy and try to see the situation from the other person's perspective. This can help you understand their motivations and reasons for their actions, which can lead to greater compassion and understanding.

Another way to work on letting go of anger and resentment is to practice self-compassion. Be kind to yourself and recognize that forgiveness is a journey, and it may take time to let go of negative emotions fully. Practice self-care and engage in activities that bring you joy and relaxation. This can help reduce stress and improve your overall well-being, which can, in turn, make the forgiveness process easier.

Let go of resentment: Letting go of resentment is an important step in the forgiveness process. Holding onto resentment can be detrimental to your mental and physical health, leading to increased stress and negative emotions. To let go of resentment, it's important to acknowledge your feelings and accept that what happened cannot be changed. Rather than dwelling on the past and feeling angry or resentful, try to focus on the present moment and the positive aspects of your life. This can include practicing gratitude, engaging in activities you enjoy, and spending time with supportive friends and family.

Another helpful technique for letting go of resentment is to practice empathy and compassion towards the person who wronged you. This doesn't mean condoning their behavior or excusing it, but rather acknowledging that they are human and capable of making mistakes. Try to put yourself in their shoes, understand their perspective, and consider the possibility of forgiveness as a way to move forward and heal.

It's important to note that letting go of resentment is not easy, and it can take time and effort to work through the process. It may also involve seeking support from a therapist or counselor, particularly if the resentment is deeply rooted or related to past trauma. However, it is possible to let go of resentment and find greater peace and happiness in your life with patience and persistence.

Practice empathy: Practicing empathy is an important part of forgiveness because it allows us to put ourselves in the other person's shoes and see things from their perspective. By doing this, we can better understand their actions and motivations, which can help us feel more compassion toward them and let go of any resentment we may be holding onto.

One way to practice empathy is to try to imagine what the other person may be feeling or going through. You can try to picture their experiences and challenges and consider how those might have influenced their behavior towards you. It can also be helpful to engage in open and honest communication with the other person, expressing your feelings and listening to their perspective in a non-judgmental way. This can help foster empathy and understanding on both sides and can pave the way for forgiveness.

While practicing empathy can be difficult, it can ultimately lead to greater healing and a stronger sense of compassion and forgiveness. It allows us to move beyond our own hurt and anger and to connect with others on a deeper level.

Write a letter: Writing a forgiveness letter can be a powerful tool to help you let go of resentment and move towards forgiveness. In this letter, you can express your feelings in a non-judgmental way and try to understand the other person's perspective. You can also choose to forgive them for their actions and release any negative feelings you may be holding onto. Writing a forgiveness letter is a personal and private process, so there's no need to share it with anyone if you don't want to.

In addition to writing a forgiveness letter, you can also try writing a gratitude letter. This is a letter expressing your gratitude towards the person who has hurt you, focusing on the positive aspects of your relationship rather than the negative. This can help you shift your mindset towards forgiveness and release any negative feelings you may be holding onto. Like the forgiveness letter, you can choose to send the gratitude letter or keep it for yourself.

It's important to note that forgiveness is a process, and it may take time and effort to let go of resentment fully. It's okay to take things one step at a time and practice forgiveness at your own pace. Seek support from friends, family, or a therapist if you need additional help in your journey toward forgiveness.

Practice self-forgiveness: Practicing self-forgiveness is an essential part of the forgiveness process. Often, we hold onto resentment towards ourselves for past mistakes and failures, which can prevent us from moving on and letting go. To practice self-forgiveness, it's important to acknowledge the mistake or wrongdoing and take responsibility for it. It can be helpful to reflect on what led to the mistake and identify what you would do differently in the future. Remember that making mistakes is a part of being human, and everyone makes them.

Another important aspect of self-forgiveness is being kind and compassionate to yourself. Treat yourself with the kindness and understanding you would offer a friend. Don't be too hard on yourself or dwell on your mistakes. Instead, focus on the present moment and the steps you can take to move forward. Use positive self-talk and affirmations to reprogram your mind and create a more positive mindset. Remind yourself that you are worthy of forgiveness and that it's possible to let go of the past.

In some cases, seeking support from a therapist or counselor can also be helpful in practicing self-forgiveness. They can provide guidance and support in the forgiveness process and help you develop healthy coping strategies for moving forward. Remember that self-forgiveness is a journey, and it may take time and practice to fully let go of past mistakes and move forward with a sense of peace and acceptance.

Seek support: Seeking support from others can be a helpful way to navigate the process of forgiveness. Talking through your thoughts and feelings with a trusted friend or family member can provide emotional support and help you gain perspective on the situation. A therapist or counselor can also provide guidance and support in the forgiveness process, helping you work through any difficult emotions and providing strategies for forgiveness.

In addition, support groups can be a helpful resource for those seeking forgiveness. Being surrounded by others who have experienced similar situations and feelings can provide a sense of community and validation. It can also be helpful to hear from others who have successfully navigated the forgiveness process, providing hope and inspiration for your own journey.

Ultimately, seeking support from others can help alleviate feelings of isolation and provide encouragement and motivation to continue working toward forgiveness.

Set boundaries: Forgiveness does not mean forgetting the past and allowing the same hurtful behavior to continue. It's important to set boundaries and communicate your needs to avoid being hurt again in the future.

Focus on the future: Focusing on the future is an important part of forgiveness. By directing your energy towards positive goals and new experiences, you can create a sense of purpose and motivation for the future. This helps to shift your focus away from the negative emotions and events of the past and towards a more positive, hopeful outlook.

Setting goals is a helpful way to focus on the future. Consider what you want to achieve in your personal or professional life and take steps to work towards those goals. This can help you feel empowered and in control of your life rather than feeling stuck in the past.

Another way to focus on the future is to practice gratitude. Make a conscious effort to notice and appreciate the good things in your life, no matter how small. This can help you cultivate a sense of positivity and hope for the future and can make it easier to let go of negative emotions and experiences from the past.

In conclusion, forgiveness is a powerful tool for letting go of negative emotions and moving forward in a positive direction. It's not always easy and may require practice and patience, but forgiving others and ourselves can profoundly impact our mental and emotional well-being. Whether it's through talking to a therapist, practicing self-compassion, or engaging in forgiveness exercises such as writing a letter or practicing empathy, there are many strategies we can use to cultivate forgiveness in our lives. By embracing forgiveness, we can free ourselves from the weight of the past and create space for healing and growth.

CHAPTER 17 -
MINDFUL BREATHING

Mindful breathing is a simple yet powerful technique that can help you release tension and calm your mind. To practice mindful breathing, find a comfortable and quiet place where you can sit or lie down. Close your eyes and focus your attention on your breath without trying to change it. Notice the sensations of the air moving in and out of your body, the rise and fall of your chest or belly, and the feeling of your breath moving through your nose or mouth.

As you focus on your breath, you may notice that your mind begins to wander to other thoughts or distractions. When this happens, simply bring your attention back to your breath without judgment or criticism. You may also try counting your breaths or adding a simple phrase or mantra, such as "inhale peace, exhale tension."

By practicing mindful breathing regularly, you can train your mind to let go of stress and negative emotions and increase your ability to stay present in the moment. This can lead to a greater sense of calm, clarity, and well-being.

Here are a few specific mindful breathing techniques that can help with letting go:

Belly Breathing: Belly breathing, also known as diaphragmatic breathing, is a relaxation technique that involves taking slow, deep breaths while focusing on the movement of the diaphragm. The diaphragm is a muscle located between the chest and abdomen that helps with breathing. By engaging the diaphragm, belly breathing can help to calm the body and mind, reduce stress and anxiety, and promote relaxation.

To practice belly breathing, start by finding a comfortable position, either sitting or lying down. Place one hand on your stomach and the other hand on your chest. Take a slow, deep breath in through your nose, feeling your stomach expand as you inhale. Try to keep your chest still while focusing on the movement of your diaphragm. Hold your breath for a few seconds, then exhale slowly through your mouth, feeling your stomach flatten as you exhale. Repeat this process for several minutes, taking slow, deep breaths and focusing on the sensation of your breath moving in and out of your body.

Belly breathing can be a helpful tool to use anytime you feel stressed, anxious, or overwhelmed. It can also be incorporated into a daily mindfulness or meditation practice to promote relaxation and reduce tension in the body. With regular practice, belly breathing can become a natural and effective way to let go of tension and negative emotions and promote a sense of calm and well-being.

Counting Breath: Counting breath is a simple yet effective mindfulness exercise that can help you let go of negative thoughts and emotions. To practice this technique, find a quiet and comfortable place to sit or lie down. Begin by taking a few deep breaths, focusing on the sensation of the air moving in and out of your body.

Once you feel relaxed and centered, start counting each breath. Count each inhale and exhale as one count, up to 10, and then start over again. If your mind starts to wander, simply bring your focus back to counting and start again from one.

Counting breath can be practiced for just a few minutes a day or for longer periods, depending on your preference. By focusing on counting, you can let go of distractions and worries and create a sense of calm and inner peace. With practice, counting breaths can become a powerful tool for managing stress and anxiety and promoting relaxation.

4-7-8 Breath: The 4-7-8 breath technique is a popular breathing exercise that can help reduce stress and anxiety and promote relaxation. To begin, find a comfortable seated position and relax your body.

Start by exhaling completely through your mouth, making a whooshing sound. Close your mouth and inhale silently through your nose for a count of four. Hold your breath for a count of seven. Then, exhale completely through your mouth for a count of eight, making the whooshing sound again.

Repeat this cycle for four full breaths and work up to eight cycles if you feel comfortable. This technique can help regulate your breathing and promote a sense of calm by slowing down your heart rate and reducing stress hormones in the body.

It is important to note that if you have any respiratory condition, such as asthma or COPD, you should check with your doctor before attempting any breathing exercises. Additionally, if you feel lightheaded or uncomfortable during the exercise, stop and return to your normal breathing.

One-Minute Breath: One-Minute Breath is a breathing exercise that is used to calm and focus the mind. It is a simple but effective practice involving inhaling, holding, and exhaling the breath for equal time. To perform this exercise, sit comfortably and close your eyes. Take a deep breath in through your nose for 20 seconds, filling your lungs with air. Hold your breath for another 20 seconds, and then exhale slowly for 20 seconds, emptying your lungs completely. Repeat this cycle for one minute or as long as you feel comfortable.

The One-Minute Breath is often used in meditation and mindfulness practices, as it helps to slow down the mind and body, reduce stress and anxiety, and improve focus and concentration. It can be done anywhere, at any time, and only requires a few minutes of your day. With regular practice, this breathing exercise can become a powerful tool for managing stress and promoting overall well-being.

Alternate Nostril Breathing: Alternate Nostril Breathing, also known as Nadi Shodhana Pranayama, is a yogic breathing technique that is said to bring balance and calmness to the body and mind. The technique involves breathing through one nostril at a time, using the fingers to alternate between the left and right nostrils.

To practice Alternate Nostril Breathing, sit in a comfortable position with your spine straight, and your eyes closed. Rest your left hand on your left knee with your palm facing up and bring your right hand to your nose.

Using your right thumb, close your right nostril and inhale deeply through your left nostril. Hold your breath for a few seconds, then release your right nostril and use your ring finger to close your left nostril. Exhale slowly through your right nostril.

Next, inhale deeply through your right nostril, hold your breath for a few seconds, then release your left nostril and exhale slowly through your left nostril. This completes one round of Alternate Nostril Breathing.

Repeat this process for several rounds, focusing on the sensation of the breath moving through each nostril. This practice can help calm the mind, reduce stress and anxiety, and promote a sense of relaxation and balance in the body.

Body Scan Meditation: Body scan meditation is a mindfulness practice that focuses on each part of your body and notices any sensations or feelings in that area. This practice aims to become more aware of your body and relax from tension or discomfort. To begin the practice, find a quiet and comfortable place to lie down, such as a yoga mat or bed. You can also sit in a comfortable chair if lying down is uncomfortable.

Start by taking a few deep breaths and settling into your body. Then, bring your attention to your toes and notice any sensations in this area. Allow any tension or discomfort to dissolve as you consciously relax your toes. Move up to your feet, ankles, and legs, and continue to relax each area as you go. Bring your awareness to your hips, lower back, and upper back, relaxing each area and noticing any sensations present.

Continue up to your shoulders, arms, and hands, allowing each area to relax completely. Finally, bring your attention to your neck, face, and head, relaxing any tension in these areas as well. Take a few deep breaths and allow yourself to relax into your body fully. This practice can be done for a few minutes or for a longer period of time, depending on your preference.

S.T.O.P. Method: Stop what you're doing, Take a deep breath, Observe your thoughts and feelings, and Proceed with what you were doing. The S.T.O.P method is a mindfulness technique that can help you pause and gain perspective when you're feeling overwhelmed or stressed. The first step is to stop what you're doing and take a few deep breaths. This can help you shift your focus from your thoughts to your breath, which can be calming and grounding.

Once you've paused and taken a few breaths, the next step is to observe your thoughts and feelings without judgment. This means simply noticing what's happening inside you without trying to change or fix it. You might notice physical sensations, emotions, or thoughts that are racing through your mind.

Finally, the last step is to proceed with what you were doing, but with a new sense of awareness and presence. By taking a moment to pause and observe your thoughts and feelings, you may be able to approach the situation with a clearer mind and a calmer demeanor.

The S.T.O.P method can be used in a variety of situations, from everyday stressors to more intense emotional experiences. It can help you gain perspective, reduce anxiety, and approach situations with greater mindfulness and awareness.

Mindful breathing techniques can be powerful tools to help us let go of negative emotions and tension and bring us into the present moment. Whether you practice belly breathing, counting breaths, or alternate nostril breathing, focusing on your breath can help calm your mind and reduce stress. With regular practice, mindful breathing can become a natural part of your daily routine, helping you to feel more centered and balanced throughout the day. So, take a moment to breathe deeply and let go of any tension or negative thoughts that may be weighing you down.

CHAPTER 18 - TALK THERAPY

Talk therapy, also known as psychotherapy, is a form of mental health treatment that involves talking to a trained therapist or counselor about your thoughts, emotions, and behaviors. Talk therapy can be a helpful way to process difficult emotions and experiences and to learn new coping strategies and problem-solving skills.

In therapy, you may work with your therapist to identify negative thought patterns or beliefs that may be contributing to your distress. For example, you may have a belief that you are not good enough or that people will always disappoint you. Your therapist can help you challenge and reframe those beliefs and develop more positive and realistic ways of thinking.

Through talk therapy, you can also learn new coping strategies for managing stress, anxiety, and depression. Your therapist may teach you relaxation, mindfulness, or cognitive-behavioral techniques to help you change your thoughts and behaviors. Overall, talk therapy can be a powerful tool for promoting emotional healing and personal growth.

Here are a few specific talk therapy techniques that can help with letting go:

Practice mindfulness: When working with a therapist or counselor, mindfulness can be incorporated into the therapy process in a number of ways. The therapist may guide the client through mindfulness exercises, such as deep breathing or body scans, to help them stay present in the moment and let go of past or future worries.

Additionally, the therapist may help the client identify negative thought patterns or beliefs that may be holding them back and work with them to challenge and reframe those thoughts to promote a more positive outlook. This can involve practicing mindfulness to help the client become more aware of their thoughts and emotions and to develop a more objective and non-judgmental perspective.

Mindfulness can also be incorporated into other therapeutic techniques, such as cognitive-behavioral therapy or acceptance and commitment therapy. In these approaches, the therapist may help the client learn to observe and accept their thoughts and emotions without judgment and to focus on the present moment rather than dwelling on the past or worrying about the future.

Role-play: Role-play is a technique used in talk therapy that can help individuals practice new ways of thinking and behaving in a safe and supportive environment. It involves simulating a real-life situation with the therapist or a trusted person playing the role of the other person involved. This technique can be particularly helpful in practicing difficult conversations or confrontations with others and building confidence in letting go of past hurts.

During a role-play, the therapist may guide the individual in exploring different ways of expressing their feelings, thoughts, and needs in a constructive and assertive manner. This can help the individual feel more prepared and confident in real-life situations, as well as help them let go of any lingering negative emotions from past experiences.

Role-play can also be useful in practicing forgiveness, as the individual can explore different perspectives and practice empathy towards the person who hurt them. By role-playing forgiving the other person, the individual can build a sense of compassion and empathy, which can help in the process of letting go and moving on.

Create an action plan: Creating an action plan with your therapist can help you set achievable goals and identify practical steps to let go of negative experiences and relationships. This may involve setting boundaries with certain people, practicing self-care and self-compassion, or working on reframing negative thought patterns. Your therapist can help you identify the most effective actions for your individual situation and needs.

Having a clear plan in place can also provide a sense of structure and purpose, which can be helpful when working through difficult emotions. Your therapist can help you break down your goals into manageable steps and provide support and accountability as you work toward them.

Creating an action plan can also help you feel more empowered and in control of your life. By identifying specific actions, you can take to let go of negative experiences and move forward, and you can start to take active steps toward a more positive and fulfilling future.

Cognitive-behavioral therapy (CBT): Cognitive-behavioral therapy (CBT) is a type of talk therapy that is often used to help individuals with mental health issues, including anxiety and depression. CBT is based on the idea that our thoughts, feelings, and behaviors are interconnected and that changing one of these components can lead to changes in the others. In CBT, the therapist works with the individual to identify negative patterns of thought and behavior that may be contributing to their distress.

Through CBT, individuals learn to identify and challenge negative thoughts, such as overgeneralization or catastrophizing, and replace them with more balanced and realistic thoughts. This can help them to feel less anxious or depressed and to develop more effective coping strategies. CBT often involves homework assignments and practice exercises, such as keeping a thought diary or practicing relaxation techniques.

Overall, CBT is a structured and evidence-based approach to talk therapy that has been shown to be effective in treating a range of mental health issues. It can help individuals to let go of negative thought patterns and develop more positive and adaptive ways of thinking and behaving.

Emotion-focused therapy (EFT): Emotion-focused therapy (EFT) is a form of talk therapy that aims to help individuals recognize, understand, and manage their emotions in a healthy way. EFT is based on the idea that emotions are essential to the human experience and that learning to manage them effectively can lead to a more fulfilling life. EFT is often used to treat conditions such as depression, anxiety, and trauma.

During EFT sessions, the therapist works with the client to identify specific emotions and the triggers that cause them. The therapist then helps the client to understand the root causes of these emotions and to develop coping strategies for managing them. EFT typically involves a combination of talk therapy, mindfulness techniques, and relaxation exercises.

One of the main goals of EFT is to help individuals develop a greater sense of emotional awareness and regulation. By learning to recognize and manage their emotions in a healthy way, individuals can reduce feelings of anxiety and depression, improve their relationships, and increase their overall sense of well-being.

Narrative therapy: Narrative therapy is a type of talk therapy that emphasizes the power of stories and the role they play in shaping our understanding of ourselves and our experiences. In narrative therapy, the therapist works with the client to identify the stories they tell themselves about their lives and how these stories influence their beliefs and behaviors. By examining these stories and exploring alternative perspectives, clients can gain greater agency and control over their lives.

The goal of narrative therapy is to help clients create a new, more positive narrative about their lives, one that emphasizes their strengths and resilience rather than their problems and limitations. This can involve re-examining past experiences and reframing them in a more positive light, as well as identifying and challenging negative self-talk and limiting beliefs.

Narrative therapy can be particularly helpful for individuals who feel stuck or overwhelmed by negative patterns in their lives or struggle with identity and self-esteem issues. It can also be useful in addressing issues related to trauma and helping clients find a sense of meaning and purpose in their lives.

Support groups: Support groups can offer a sense of community and belonging, which can be especially valuable for individuals who may feel isolated or alone in their struggles. It can be helpful to hear from others who have been through similar experiences and have come out on the other side. In a support group, you may find validation for your feelings and new coping strategies and perspectives.

Support groups can take many forms, including online forums, in-person meetings, or group therapy sessions. It can be helpful to find a group that is focused on your specific struggle or experience, such as a group for individuals who have experienced trauma, a group for people going through a divorce, or a group for those struggling with addiction.

Participating in a support group can also provide a sense of accountability, as members may hold each other accountable for working towards their goals and making positive changes in their lives. It can be empowering to see the progress of others in the group and to feel that you are part of a community that is working towards similar goals.

In conclusion, talk therapy is a powerful tool for individuals seeking to let go of negative emotions, experiences, or relationships. Through various therapeutic approaches, including cognitive-behavioral therapy, emotion-focused therapy, narrative therapy, and role-play, individuals can learn to identify and challenge negative patterns of thought and behavior, manage difficult emotions, reframe their narrative, and create an action plan for moving forward in a positive direction. Additionally, support groups provide a valuable space for individuals to connect with others who may be going through similar struggles, learn from their experiences, and gain support and encouragement to let go and move forward. Seeking support from a therapist or support group can be an important step towards letting go and finding greater peace and happiness in life.

CHAPTER 19 - LETTING GO RITUAL

A letting go ritual can be a powerful emotional healing and transformation tool. Creating a ritual can help us acknowledge our pain, give us a sense of closure, and symbolically let go of negative thoughts and emotions that are holding us back. The ritual can be a private, personal act or shared with others, depending on what feels most comfortable and appropriate for the individual.

One common letting go ritual involves writing down negative thoughts or emotions on a piece of paper and then burning the paper to symbolize releasing those feelings. This can be done in a quiet, meditative space or as part of a group ceremony. Another ritual involves tossing stones or other objects into a body of water and letting go of negative thoughts and emotions with each throw.

Whatever form the letting go ritual takes, it can be a powerful way to bring closure to a difficult experience and start the process of moving on. By acknowledging our pain and releasing negative emotions, we create space for healing and growth and can move forward with a renewed sense of purpose and positivity.

Here are a few specific 'letting go ritual' techniques that can help with letting go:

Write down what you want to let go of: Writing down what you want to let go of can be a powerful step towards releasing negative thoughts and emotions. It allows you to identify and acknowledge the things holding you back and helps you take ownership of your emotions. When writing down what you want to let go of, it's important to be specific and honest with yourself. Don't hold back, and don't judge yourself for the things you write down.

Once you've written down what you want to let go of, you can choose to do different things with the paper. Some people find it helpful to rip the paper up into small pieces and throw them away, symbolizing the act of letting go. Others may choose to burn the paper, watching the negative emotions or thoughts disappear into smoke. You can also keep the paper as a reminder of what you've overcome and what you're working towards letting go of.

The act of writing down what you want to let go of can be a cathartic experience, allowing you to release emotions that may have been bottled up inside. It's a simple yet powerful tool that can be part of a larger process of letting go and moving toward a happier, healthier life.

Choose a symbolic action: Choosing a symbolic action can help make the act of letting go more tangible and real. It provides a physical representation of the release you're seeking. You can choose an action that feels most meaningful to you or one that relates to the specific thing you're letting go of. For example, if you're letting go of a relationship, you may burn the paper to symbolically release that person from your life.

When choosing a symbolic action, it's important to remember that the act itself is not what's important; it's the intention behind it. The action simply serves as a visual representation of your commitment to let go and move forward. So, choose an action that feels authentic to you and resonates with your beliefs and values.

After choosing your symbolic action, take a moment to visualize yourself letting go of the negative emotions or beliefs you've written down. See yourself releasing them and feel a sense of relief and peace. Then, take the symbolic action and take a deep breath, knowing you've taken a step toward healing and growth.

Find a quiet space: Finding a quiet space is essential to perform the letting go ritual with mindfulness and intention. When we are surrounded by noise or distraction, it can be challenging to focus on our thoughts and feelings. Therefore, it is best to find a place where we feel comfortable and safe and let ourselves be vulnerable without interruption.

The quiet space can be anywhere, allowing you to feel relaxed and peaceful. For some people, this might mean being in nature; for others, it could be a quiet room at home or a meditation center. The key is to find a space that works for you, where you can focus on your thoughts and emotions without any external distractions.

Once you've found your quiet space, take a moment to get comfortable and relax. You may want to light a candle, burn incense, or play soothing music to help create a calming atmosphere. Allow yourself to settle into the space and feel your body and mind become more centered and present.

By finding a quiet space, we create an environment that allows us to be fully present in the moment and focus on our intentions. This is essential for the letting go ritual to be effective and meaningful.

Focus on your breath: Focusing on your breath is key to many mindfulness practices, including letting go rituals. By paying attention to your breath, you can become more present and centered and let go of distracting thoughts and emotions. Take a few deep breaths in through your nose, filling your lungs with air, and exhale slowly through your mouth, releasing any tension or stress. Allow your breath to become slow and steady, and let it guide you toward a state of relaxation and calm.

If you find your mind wandering, gently bring your focus

back to your breath. Notice the sensation of the air moving in and out of your nostrils or the rise and fall of your chest and abdomen. With each inhale, imagine yourself breathing in peace, love, and positive energy. With each exhale, imagine yourself releasing negative emotions and thoughts. Use your breath as an anchor to bring you back to the present moment and let go of anything that's holding you back.

By focusing on your breath and letting go of distracting thoughts and emotions, you can create a space for clarity and insight. This can help you gain a new perspective on the things you want to let go of and find the strength and courage to move forward in a positive direction.

Read your list out loud: Reading your list out loud can help bring awareness and acknowledgment to the things you want to let go of. It can also help you identify any emotions or feelings that may come up as you read the list. This process can be cathartic and help you release any pent-up emotions related to these things.

As you read each item, try to approach it with a sense of detachment and non-judgment. Simply observe the thoughts and emotions that arise and allow yourself to feel them without getting caught up in them. Remember that this is a process, and it's okay to take your time and work through your feelings at your own pace.

It can also be helpful to have a trusted friend or therapist present during this process to provide support and guidance or to simply be a listening ear.

Overall, reading your list out loud is an important step in the letting go process. It can help you acknowledge and release negative emotions and move forward toward a more positive and fulfilling life.

Perform your symbolic action: Performing your symbolic action is an important step in the letting go ritual as it helps to reinforce the intention of letting go. The symbolic action you choose should be meaningful to you and represent the release of negative emotions, habits, or relationships you want to let go of.

For example, if you wrote down negative thoughts or beliefs that you want to let go of, you could choose to burn the paper. As you watch the paper burn, you can visualize those negative thoughts and beliefs leaving your mind and body and being replaced by positive, empowering thoughts.

If you wrote down a toxic relationship that you want to let go of, you could choose to release a balloon or a bird to symbolize the relationship flying away from you. As you watch the balloon or bird fly away, you can visualize yourself being free from the negative emotions associated with that relationship and feeling lighter and happier.

Whatever symbolic action you choose, it's important to focus on the intention behind it and to visualize yourself letting go of the things on your list. This can help you feel more empowered and in control of your thoughts and emotions, leading to a greater sense of inner peace and contentment.

Repeat a mantra or affirmation: Repeating a mantra or affirmation can help solidify the process of letting go and moving forward with positivity. The mantra can be simple phrases such as "I release and let go" or "I am open to new possibilities." It should be something that resonates with you and your goals for letting go.

By repeating the mantra or affirmation, you are creating a new positive belief system that replaces the negative beliefs and emotions you are letting go of. It can help you shift your focus to a more positive mindset and reinforce your commitment to moving forward.

You can repeat your chosen mantra or affirmation silently to yourself or out loud if you prefer. Repeat it several times, and really focus on the words and the feeling behind them. Allow yourself to feel the power of the words and the intention behind them.

Remember that the process of letting go and moving forward is a journey, and it may take time to let go of negative emotions and beliefs fully. But by incorporating a mantra or affirmation into your letting go ritual, you are setting yourself up for success and creating a positive foundation for your future growth and development.

Take time for self-care: After completing your letting go ritual, it's important to take some time for self-care. Letting go of negative emotions and beliefs can be emotionally taxing, and it's important to prioritize your own well-being in the aftermath. There are many ways to practice self-care, and it's important to find what works best for you.

One simple way to practice self-care is to take a warm bath or shower. The warm water can help soothe your muscles and calm your mind. You could also light candles or use aromatherapy to create a relaxing environment.

Meditation is another powerful self-care practice that can help you connect with your inner self and find peace and clarity. You can practice meditation on your own or use guided meditations available online or through meditation apps.

Yoga is another great self-care practice that can help you release tension and connect with your body. You can find yoga classes online or in person or practice on your own with videos or books.

Finally, it's important to remember that self-care is not just about physical practices but also about emotional and mental well-being. Take time to reflect on your feelings and thoughts and talk to a trusted friend or therapist if you need support. Remember to be kind and compassionate to yourself throughout the process of letting go and moving forward.

In conclusion, creating a letting go ritual can be a powerful way to release negative emotions and beliefs that are holding us back. By writing down what we want to let go of, choosing a symbolic action, and performing the ritual in a quiet space, we can begin to release the weight of our negative thoughts and emotions. By focusing on our breath, reading our list out loud, and repeating a positive mantra or affirmation, we can reinforce our commitment to letting go and moving forward with a new beginning.

It's important to take time for self-care after the ritual, whether it's through meditation, yoga, or another form of relaxation. By committing to this process and honoring our emotions, we can begin to cultivate a sense of peace and renewal, letting go of the past and embracing the present moment

CHAPTER 20 – ACCEPTANCE

Acceptance is an important part of the process of letting go. It involves acknowledging the reality of a situation and understanding that some things are beyond our control. This can be difficult, especially when we're faced with challenges or disappointments. But by accepting the things we cannot change, we can begin to focus on what we can control.

Acceptance doesn't mean giving up or resigning ourselves to a negative situation. Instead, it's about acknowledging reality and shifting our focus to what we can do to move forward in a positive direction. This may involve setting new goals or finding new ways to approach a problem. It can also involve reframing our thoughts and beliefs about a situation.

Practicing acceptance can be challenging, but it can also be liberating. By accepting what we cannot change, we can let go of the stress and negative emotions that come with trying to control things that are beyond our control. This can free up energy and mental space for more positive pursuits and can ultimately lead to greater peace and happiness.

Here are a few specific acceptance techniques that can help with letting go:

Mindful awareness: Mindful awareness can be a helpful practice in cultivating acceptance. By learning to observe our thoughts and emotions without judgment, we can become more aware of what we can and cannot control. This allows us to let go of the urge to fight or resist situations that are beyond our control and instead focus on what we can do to respond healthily and productively.

When we practice mindful awareness, we become more attuned to our thoughts and feelings and recognize when we struggle with acceptance. We can observe our internal dialogue and notice when we're stuck in a pattern of resistance or denial. With this awareness, we can begin to shift our mindset and move toward acceptance.

By accepting what we cannot change, we can reduce our stress and anxiety and free up energy to focus on what we can control. This doesn't mean that we give up or stop striving for change, but rather that we let go of the frustration and negativity that can come from trying to control the uncontrollable. Instead, we can focus on taking action toward positive change in areas where we do have agency and influence.

Overall, practicing mindful awareness can help us cultivate a mindset of acceptance, which can lead to greater peace and resilience in the face of life's challenges.

Reframing: Reframing is a powerful tool in practicing acceptance. It involves shifting our perspective on a situation or event from a negative to a more positive one. This can help us see challenges as opportunities for growth and learning rather than as roadblocks or failures.

One way to reframe negative thoughts is to practice gratitude. By focusing on the positive aspects of our lives, we can shift our attention away from what we cannot change and towards what we have control over. This can help us feel more empowered and optimistic about the future.

Another way to reframe negative thoughts is to challenge negative self-talk. We often have automatic negative thoughts that can hold us back and make us feel worse. By recognizing these thoughts and challenging them with evidence or more positive alternatives, we can reframe our thinking and feel more positive and accepting.

Overall, practicing acceptance through reframing can help us let go of stress and negative emotions related to circumstances beyond our control. By focusing on what we can control and reframing negative thoughts, we can find peace and contentment in the present moment.

Self-compassion: Self-compassion involves treating ourselves with kindness and understanding when we face difficult emotions or challenging situations. It's a way of being supportive and gentle with ourselves rather than being overly critical or harsh. When we practice self-compassion, we acknowledge that we are human and that it's normal to struggle at times. By doing so, we can reduce our suffering and increase our well-being.

To practice self-compassion, we can start by becoming aware of the ways in which we talk to ourselves. We may tend to judge ourselves harshly or be overly critical, which can increase our stress levels and undermine our self-esteem. Instead, we can cultivate a more supportive inner voice that encourages us and helps us feel more confident and capable.

We can also practice self-compassion by treating ourselves with kindness and care. This may involve taking time for self-care activities like taking a relaxing bath, going for a walk in nature, or practicing yoga or meditation. We can also prioritize our needs and set healthy boundaries with others, recognizing that our well-being is important.

In moments of difficulty or pain, we can practice self-compassion by acknowledging our feelings without judging or suppressing them. Instead of trying to push away our difficult emotions, we can give ourselves permission to feel them and offer ourselves words of comfort and support. This can help us feel more connected to ourselves and reduce feelings of loneliness or isolation.

Letting go of control: Letting go of control is an

important aspect of acceptance. It can be difficult to accept that we cannot control everything in our lives, but acknowledging this fact can help us let go of stress and anxiety related to trying to control the uncontrollable. It can also help us focus our energy on the things we can control and take action to make positive changes in those areas.

Letting go of control can involve practicing mindfulness and learning to let go of thoughts and feelings without judgment. It can also involve reframing negative thoughts and focusing on the positive aspects of a situation. Additionally, it can be helpful to practice self-compassion and treat ourselves with kindness and understanding when things don't go according to plan.

Learning to let go of control can be challenging, but it can ultimately lead to greater peace of mind and a sense of acceptance. By recognizing our limitations and focusing on what we can control, we can let go of stress and negative emotions and embrace a more positive outlook on life.

Gratitude: Gratitude is a powerful tool for cultivating a positive mindset and increasing feelings of well-being. When we focus on what we are grateful for, we shift our attention away from negative thoughts and emotions and instead focus on the positive aspects of our lives. Gratitude helps us recognize and appreciate the good things we have, improving our overall outlook and increasing our resilience in the face of challenges.

There are many ways to practice gratitude, such as keeping a gratitude journal, saying thank you to others, or simply taking time to appreciate the beauty of nature. Making gratitude a regular part of our lives can help us feel more positive, reduce stress, and build stronger relationships with others.

Gratitude can also help us let go of negative emotions by focusing on what we have rather than what we lack. When we are grateful for what we have, we are less likely to feel jealous or envious of others and more likely to feel content and fulfilled. By focusing on the positive aspects of our lives, we can let go of negative emotions and cultivate a more positive outlook.

Focus on the present: Focusing on the present can help us let go of stress and anxiety about things we cannot control. It allows us to fully engage with what is happening around us and appreciate the small moments of joy we might otherwise overlook. One way to focus on the present is to engage in mindfulness practices, such as meditation, deep breathing, or body scans. These techniques help us tune out distractions and bring our attention back to the present moment.

Another way to focus on the present is to engage in activities that require our full attention and concentration, such as exercise, art, or cooking. By immersing ourselves in these activities, we can let go of worries and concerns about the past or future and fully embrace the present moment. This can help us feel more connected to ourselves and the world around us, leading to a greater sense of peace and contentment.

It's important to remember that focusing on the present doesn't mean ignoring the past or disregarding the future. Rather, it means being mindful and intentional in our thoughts and actions and acknowledging that the present is the only moment we have control over. By staying present and engaged, we can let go of stress and negative emotions and cultivate a greater sense of happiness and well-being.

Mindful breathing: Mindful breathing is a powerful tool for accepting the present moment and letting go of stress and negative thoughts. By bringing your attention to your breath, you can ground yourself in the present moment and cultivate a sense of calm and relaxation. Mindful breathing involves paying attention to your breath as it moves in and out of your body without judgment or the need to control it.

One effective mindful breathing technique is to focus on the sensation of the breath as it moves through your body. You can do this by placing one hand on your chest and the other on your stomach and feeling the rise and fall of your breath. As you inhale, imagine the breath flowing into your body; as you exhale, imagine it flowing out. If your mind wanders, gently bring your focus back to your breath.

Another technique is to count your breaths. This involves counting each inhale and exhale up to a certain number, such as 10, and then starting over again. If your mind wanders, simply bring your focus back to counting.

Through regular practice of mindful breathing, you can learn to accept the present moment as it is, without judgment or the need to control it. This can help you cultivate a sense of peace and calm and let go of stress and negative emotions.

Cognitive-behavioral techniques: Cognitive-behavioral techniques can be especially useful when it comes to acceptance. By learning to identify and challenge negative thoughts, we can shift our perspective and approach difficult situations with greater clarity and resilience. Cognitive-behavioral therapy (CBT) is a form of talk therapy that can help us recognize and change negative patterns of thought and behavior. With the help of a trained therapist, we can learn strategies to identify and challenge negative thoughts and replace them with more positive ones.

CBT can help us develop more positive coping skills, such as mindfulness, self-compassion, and reframing negative experiences. By focusing on what we can control and accepting what we cannot, we can let go of stress and negative emotions related to circumstances beyond our control. CBT can also help us learn to communicate more effectively and assertively, especially when dealing with difficult relationships or situations.

In addition to CBT, other forms of talk therapy, such as acceptance and commitment therapy (ACT) or mindfulness-based stress reduction (MBSR), can also be effective in cultivating acceptance. These therapies focus on developing mindfulness and acceptance as core skills for coping with difficult emotions and experiences. Through these therapies, we can learn to observe our thoughts and feelings without judgment and cultivate a more compassionate and accepting relationship with ourselves and the world around us.

Support system: Having a strong support system can be essential when practicing acceptance, as it can provide the encouragement and guidance needed to work through difficult emotions and situations. Consider reaching out to friends or family members who are supportive and non-judgmental and who can offer a listening ear and practical help when needed. Alternatively, consider working with a therapist or counselor who can provide specialized support and guidance.

Therapy can be especially helpful when working on practicing acceptance, as a therapist can help you identify negative thought patterns and behaviors that may be holding you back and offer strategies to develop more positive coping skills. Cognitive-behavioral therapy (CBT), for example, is a type of talk therapy that focuses on changing negative patterns of thought and behavior.

In addition to therapy, support groups are available that can offer a sense of community and belonging. Consider joining a support group that is focused on acceptance or a related topic, such as mindfulness or self-compassion. This can provide an opportunity to connect with others who are going through similar experiences and share tips and advice on practicing acceptance.

Letting go ritual: Create a letting go ritual to help you physically and symbolically release negative thoughts or feelings. This could involve writing them down, burning the paper, or releasing a symbolic object into nature.

Letting go of negative thoughts, emotions, and beliefs can

be challenging, but it's an essential part of personal growth and transformation. The obstacles we face in letting go are often rooted in fear, whether fear of the unknown, loss, or judgment. However, by practicing practical techniques such as mindfulness, self-compassion, and reframing, we can learn to let go of what no longer serves us and create space for new opportunities and experiences.

Remember that letting go is a process, and it takes time and effort to cultivate a mindset of acceptance and openness. Be patient and kind to yourself as you navigate this journey, and know that it's okay to ask for help and support along the way. By letting go, you can create a more fulfilling and meaningful life for yourself, filled with joy, gratitude, and love.

CHAPTER 21 – CONCLUSION

Letting go is an essential aspect of our emotional well-being, which allows us to move past previous hurts and negative emotions, freeing up our mental and emotional resources for more positive endeavors. It is an ongoing process that requires attention, effort, and dedication, but the benefits of letting go are invaluable. By practicing techniques like mindfulness, visualization exercises, gratitude, self-care, and acceptance, we can begin to release negative thoughts and emotions and create space for more positive and fulfilling experiences.

Letting go can bring inner peace, reduce stress and anxiety, improve relationships, and increase self-awareness. It can also help us cultivate creativity and innovation as we learn to approach challenges with an open mind and a positive attitude. Through cognitive-behavioral techniques and the support of our social networks, we can also work to change negative thought patterns and develop positive coping skills, further enhancing our ability to let go and move forward.

The process of letting go is not always easy, and it may require patience and persistence. However, with practice and dedication, we can learn to let go of the past and focus on the present moment, enjoying all that life has to offer. Ultimately, by letting go of negative thoughts and emotions, we can live a more fulfilling and meaningful life full of joy, peace, and purpose.

Throughout this book, we've explored the principles of

letting go, including understanding what it means to let go, recognizing the obstacles to letting go, practical techniques for letting go, and how to apply the principles of letting go in daily life. We've also explored the benefits of letting go and how it can help us create a more fulfilling and joyful life for ourselves and those around us.

It's important to remember that the process of letting go is not always easy or straightforward. It can be a journey that requires time, patience, and practice. We may need to let go of things that have been a part of our lives for a long time, and it can be challenging to release something that has become familiar, even if it's causing us pain or stress. But with self-compassion and a willingness to work on ourselves, we can learn how to let go and move forward towards a more positive and fulfilling life.

As we've discussed, many tools and techniques are available to help us let go, such as mindfulness meditation, cognitive-behavioral therapy, visualization exercises, gratitude practice, and self-care. We can also create a letting go ritual or seek support from a therapist or support group. It's important to find the best approach for us and be open to trying new things as we continue to let go.

By letting go of what's holding us back, we can create more space in our lives for the things that bring us joy, meaning, and fulfillment. We can become more self-aware, build stronger relationships, and cultivate a greater sense of inner peace and contentment. Remember that letting go is a process, but with time, effort, and a willingness to practice, we can create the positive changes we seek in our lives.

Letting go of what's holding you back is essential for personal growth and development. Holding onto negative emotions, past mistakes, or toxic relationships can prevent us from moving forward in life and experiencing the full potential of our happiness and success. It's important to recognize that letting go is not a one-time event but rather a continuous process that requires conscious effort and commitment.

By letting go, we create space for new possibilities and opportunities to emerge. We become open to new experiences and relationships, and our mindset shifts towards positivity and optimism. Instead of being stuck in the past or worrying about the future, we learn to live in the present moment and appreciate the beauty of life as it unfolds.

Embracing the possibilities and opportunities that await us requires courage and a willingness to step outside of our comfort zone. It's important to remember that growth and change can be uncomfortable at times, but the rewards are well worth it. By letting go of what's holding us back, we create the space to discover new passions, achieve our goals, and ultimately live a more fulfilling and meaningful life.

So, if you're ready to embark on a journey toward greater inner peace and happiness, start by letting go of what's no longer serving you. Embrace the possibilities and opportunities that await you with an open heart and a positive mindset. Your journey towards a more fulfilling life starts now.

www.ingramcontent.com/pod-product-compliance
Lightning Source LLC
La Vergne TN
LVHW051254080426
835509LV00020B/2973